W9-BYY-035

OCEANOGRAPHERS
AND EXPLORERS
OF THE SEA

Other titles in the **Collective Biographies** *series*

Collective Biographies

OCEANOGRAPHERS AND EXPLORERS OF THE SEA

Kirk Polking

Discard

NHCPL

NEW HANOVER COUNTY
PUBLIC LIBRARY
201 CHESTNUT STREET
WILMINGTON, NC 28401

Enslow Publishers, Inc.

40 Industrial Road	PO Box 38
Box 398	Aldershot
Berkeley Heights, NJ 07922	Hants GU12 6BP
USA	UK

http://www.enslow.com

Copyright © 1999 by Kirk Polking

All rights reserved.

No part of this book may be reproduced by any means
without the written permission of the publisher.

Library of Congress Cataloging-in-Publication Data

Polking, Kirk.
    Oceanographers and explorers of the sea / Kirk Polking
       p. cm. — (Collective biographies)
    Includes bibliographical references and index.
    Summary: Biographies of ten scientists who studied the ocean,
including physicists, environmentalists, geologists, and biologists.
    ISBN 0-7660-1113-5
      1. Oceanographers—United States—Biography—Juvenile literature.
    2. Explorers—United States—Biography—Juvenile literature.
    3. Scientists—United States—Biography—Juvenile literature.
    [1. Oceanographers. 2. Explorers. 3. Scientists.] I. Title.
    II. Series.
    GC30.A1P65   1999
    551.46'0092'2—dc21
    [B]   98-36135
                                          CIP
                                          AC

Printed in the United States of America

10 9 8 7 6 5 4 3 2

To Our Readers:
All Internet addresses in this book were active and appropriate when we went to press.
Any comments or suggestions can be sent by e-mail to Comments@enslow.com or to
the address on the back cover.

Illustration Credits: Andreas Rechnitzer, p. 62; Courtesy of Al
Giddings/Deep Ocean Exploration and Research, p. 38; Courtesy of Deep
Ocean Exploration and Research, p. 32; Reproduced with permission from
the Institute for Exploration, p. 92; Jeff Cordia, Scripps Institution of
Oceanography, p. 54; From Just, E.E. 1919. Biological Bulletin 36: 1–10.
Marine Biological Laboratory, Woods Hole, Mass., p. 29; Marine Biological
Laboratory, p. 22; NASA, pp. 102, 109; Scripps Institution of
Oceanography, pp. 42, 50; University of Maryland, p. 69; The University of
Texas Institute for Geophysics, p. 12; U.S. Naval Oceanographic Office, pp.
19, 79; Walter Munk, Scripps Institution of Oceanography, p. 58; Woods
Hole Oceanographic Institution, pp. 74, 82, 85, 99.

Cover Illustration: JASON Foundation for Education

Contents

Acknowledgments

The author acknowledges the help of the following persons: Robert Ballard, Eugenie Clark, Sylvia Earle, Walter Munk, Mrs. Henry Stommel, Kathryn Sullivan, and Mrs. Allyn Vine; Vicky Cullen, Margot Garritt, Nelson Hogg, Shelley Lauzon, and Kathy Patterson, Woods Hole Oceanographic Institution; Paige Jennings, Carolyn Rainey, Deborah Day, Cindy Clark, and Breck Betts, Scripps Institution of Oceanography; William B. F. Ryan and Faye Yates, Lamont-Doherty Earth Observatory; Beth Liles, Marine Biological Laboratory; George M. Langford, Dartmouth; Deb Adamson and Annette White, Institute for Exploration; Gail Cleere, Office of the Oceanographer of the Navy; Gary Weir, Naval Historical Center; William Lescure, Office of Naval Research; Kathryn Townsend and Gerald Leone, Naval Oceanographic Office; Jennifer Geisler, American Geophysical Union; Richard W. Spinrad, Consortium for Oceanographic Research and Education; Cheryl Russell, NOAA; Emmy Scammahorn and Barbara Moffet, National Geographic Society; Douglas Isbell, Mike Gentry, Eileen Hawley, and Laura Rochon at NASA; Pamela Baker-Masson, Joint Oceanographic Institutions; Maria Gallagher, JASON Foundation; Steven Katona, College of the Atlantic; William Carey, *IEEE Journal of Oceanic Engineering*; Eli Joel Katz, *Journal of Physical Oceanography*; Michael Cruickshank, Marine Minerals Technology Center; Martin Finerty, Marine Technology Society; David Graham, *Sea Technology Magazine*; Ann West-Valle, *Oceanography Magazine*; D. W. Bennett, *Underwater Naturalist*.

Preface

Oceanography is one of the newest sciences. Until the fifteenth and sixteenth centuries, when daring explorers such as Christopher Columbus and Ferdinand Magellan made voyages of discovery, people did not even know where all of the world's oceans were located. Now we know that the oceans cover 71 percent of the earth. The oceans drive movements of the atmosphere. Their waters allow plants, animals, and people to live. Their depths hide a mountain (Mauna Kea) higher than Everest, gorges deeper than the Grand Canyon, and millions of living things we've never seen. The oceans are the last frontier—right here on our own planet.

Scientists did not begin serious study of the ocean until the nineteenth century. Americans played an important part in advancing this science. For example, Lieutenant Matthew Fontaine Maury, head of the United States Navy's chart depot, asked ship navigators from around the world to share with him information about their sailing times and directions. By 1851 about one thousand ships were participating. Maury made charts showing ocean currents and depths. In 1855 he published some of these maps and charts in a textbook titled *The Physical Geography of the Sea*. His data helped ship captains shorten their sailing times. A ship that had formerly taken 180 days to sail from New York to San Francisco could then make the journey in only 133 days. Maury's data also indicated an ocean bottom plateau between Ireland and Newfoundland that was ideal for laying the first transatlantic telegraph cable. The telegraph was a device that sent coded messages over electric wires, used before the telephone was invented.

The first major ocean expedition to explore and investigate life in the deep sea began in 1872. This was the voyage around the world by the British ship HMS *Challenger*. The scientists aboard did not find any sea monsters, as superstitious sailors had imagined they would. But they did discover over four thousand sea animal and plant species. They published a fifty-volume report of their findings, but many mysteries of the ocean remained unsolved.

Since then, new diving equipment, computers, and other modern tools have enhanced research in the oceans. By some estimates, however, only one-tenth of one percent of the ocean has been explored. Many different kinds of scientists are now working to try to learn the ocean's secrets.

What can we learn from study of the ocean? We can learn to use the ocean wisely, which holds the key to our survival on the earth. We want to know what is in it, why it moves the way it does, and how it affects our climate. Can we take millions of the ocean's fish for food but balance our use with the food needs of marine life? Can we mine the ocean for gas and oil but not destroy its life with pollution?

Several hundred institutions now conduct research in ocean studies. Among the largest in the

United States are the Woods Hole Oceanographic Institution in Massachusetts, the Scripps Institution of Oceanography in La Jolla, California, and the Lamont-Doherty Earth Observatory in Palisades, New York. Numerous colleges and universities are also training scientists to become oceanographers. They provide the very important basic education every scientist needs. Oceanography needs more men and women—like those in this book—to help discover and solve the remaining mysteries of the ocean.

This book describes the work of ten twentieth-century American oceanographers who helped establish America's international reputation in the field of ocean science. They are physicists, geologists, marine biologists, astronauts, and environmentalists. Physicists study the energy of waves, heat, and sound in the ocean. Geologists look at the content, form, and history of the earth under the sea. Astronauts record the interaction of the earth's ocean and atmosphere. Environmentalists remind us of the role we play in the life of the ocean. These scientists are willing to do the months of tedious detailed work that goes with the occasional excitement of discovery. They keep an open mind when a favorite theory is replaced by some new development. Their expeditions to explore the ocean from top to bottom and analyze its structure and content give us new insight into the mysteries of the sea.

1

Maurice Ewing

Mapping the Ocean Floor

One afternoon in 1934, two geologists called on physics professor Maurice Ewing in his basement office at Lehigh University in Bethlehem, Pennsylvania. The visitors, Professor Richard Field of Princeton and Dr. William Bowie of the Coast and Geodetic Survey, wanted Ewing's help in mapping the continental shelf—the shallow plain that borders a continent and usually ends with a steep drop to the ocean floor. They thought it was an important geological question to determine where the edges of continents are located. Could seismic reflection methods that Ewing had been using on land to help oil drilling companies be used in the open sea? they asked. "I said yes it could be done if one had the equipment and ships. (If they had asked me to put

Maurice Ewing

seismographs on the moon instead of the bottom of the sea, I'd have agreed. I was so desperate to do research.)"[1] Ewing received a two-thousand-dollar grant from the Geological Society of America to do the initial mapping off the Virginia coast. It began a new era in oceanography. Over the next forty years, Ewing's use of seismographs in oceanographic research went beyond the continental shelf to the deep sea.

William Maurice Ewing was born May 12, 1906, in Lockney, Texas, the fourth of ten children. His father was a farmer and dealer in farm equipment. In 1922 William attended Rice Institute (now Rice University) in Houston, majoring in physics and mathematics. He received his bachelor's degree in physics in 1926 and his doctorate in 1931. Ewing married fellow student Avarilla Hildenbrand in 1928, and they had one son. Later, in 1941, Ewing and Avarilla divorced, and in 1944 he married Margaret Kidder, with whom he had four children.

During college summers, Ewing worked for oil prospecting companies, which gave him field experience in the use of seismic techniques. Oil drilling companies used explosives to release energy waves that would be reflected by underground rocks. Different rock types reflected the waves in varying wavelengths. By measuring the reflected waves, geologists could analyze the underground rock structures for oil-bearing characteristics.

After Field and Bowie came to see him, Ewing began to apply his expertise in geology and physics to study of the ocean. He was the first to use powerful sound waves created by exploding TNT to chart the ocean floor and its underlying structure. Two ships were used in the experiment. One ship sailed in a straight line, dropping charges of TNT. The sound traveled down through the water to the sea bottom and its layers of sediment and rock. The reflected sound waves were detected by hydrophones (underwater microphones) hung from a stationary listening ship. To reduce noise in the water, the listening ship's engines were silent and the listening equipment was powered by batteries. The hydrophones converted the sound to pulses of electricity, which were recorded as wiggly lines on long strips of paper.[2] Modern depth recorders send sound waves to the bottom and record depths automatically as the ship cruises through the water. Over the years Ewing continued his mapping work on several research expeditions.

In 1940, Ewing took a leave of absence from teaching physics at Lehigh to work as a research associate at the Woods Hole Oceanographic Institution. During World War II, Ewing did secret research work there for the Navy. He discovered a low-velocity channel in the ocean that carries sound for unusually great distances. This natural channel exists at certain levels in the ocean where the combination of salt content, temperature, and pressure conditions are just right. Taking advantage of this channel, Ewing created sofar (sound fixing and ranging). This method was used to rescue men from ships or planes lost at sea.

The idea for sofar first came to Ewing in 1937. He was aboard the research ship *Atlantis,* mapping the seafloor for the Navy by using small bombs to create sound waves. He noticed that simply by holding his ear to the ship's rail, he could hear bombs explode on the ocean floor three miles below. Each blast was followed by three echoes, each six seconds apart. He theorized that the echoes were caused by the existence of a natural sound channel between differing temperature and pressure levels in the ocean. He tested his theory by dropping bombs from one ship. The sound was picked up by a hydrophone suspended from a second ship one thousand miles away.[3] What started as a technique to map the ocean bottom became a valuable rescue tool. Later, it also proved useful for the work of Walter Munk and other scientists.

During World War II, Ewing and his associates, Allyn Vine and John Worzel, developed and used the first underwater cameras. The photographs they obtained showed never-before-seen characteristics of the sea bottom. Ewing, Vine, and Worzel discovered ripples in the sand caused by currents, which scientists had previously thought did not exist at the ocean bottom.

After the war, Ewing moved to Columbia University in New York City to establish a program of instruction in the geophysical study of the earth. But he remained a research associate at Woods Hole because it had research vessels. In the summer of 1947 he led his first large expedition to the Mid-Atlantic Ridge aboard the *Atlantis*. Scientists wanted to explore this chain of undersea mountains to determine when and how it was formed. They also wanted to study samples of the sea bottom to learn about the earth's climate and the life that existed millions of years ago. They lowered a steel tube with a piston inside. When the tube pierced the ocean bottom, it sucked up cores of soft sediment to study. In the sediment and fossils from the cores, the scientists found many new mysteries. For example, geologists thought that if they found evidence of the beginning of an ice age in one core, they would also find it in cores one hundred miles away. But they discovered that the conditions in the ocean at any one time were not uniform.[4] To Ewing, the findings meant one thing: Send out more ships, map the ocean bottom, study the charts, and gather enough data for scientists to propose new theories about these discoveries.

In 1949 Ewing founded what is now Columbia University's Lamont-Doherty Earth Observatory. In 1953 Lamont-Doherty obtained its first ship, called the *Vema*. The ship provided Ewing the possibility for worldwide expeditions and the chance to conduct multiple research programs at one time. Ewing's continued studies of the Mid-Atlantic Ridge took advantage of newer technologies. He and his colleagues improved the depth recorder by adding a precision clock. The improved recorder gave measurements with an accuracy within one fathom (six feet) in three thousand fathoms (eighteen thousand feet) of water.

The Mid-Atlantic Ridge was discovered when telegraph cables were first laid across the Atlantic in 1858. But it was Ewing's crew in 1956 who proved that this broad underwater mountain range extends forty thousand miles through all the oceans of the world.[5] In 1957, with the assistance of colleagues Marie Tharp and Bruce Heezen, Ewing discovered that the Mid-Atlantic Ridge is divided by a central rift. In some places this rift is twice as deep and wide as the Grand Canyon.

In another experiment, Ewing towed magnetometers behind a ship to map the earth's magnetic field along different parts of the seafloor. The magnetometer detected variations in magnetic polarity, which indicated that the earth's magnetic field shifted over time. When lava exudes from beneath the crust and solidifies, iron particles in the cooling molten rock align with the direction of the earth's magnetic field. Scientists discovered parallel stripes of alternating high and low magnetization in the volcanic rocks that make up the midocean ridges. Their locations and the dates of their formation form a record of the spreading of the ocean floor.

Ewing also measured variations in gravity along the ocean floor. Using a gravity meter, which measures gravitational attraction (the tug on the ship by the earth's mass beneath it), Ewing discovered that the attraction over deep ocean trenches was weaker than expected. Using other measurements of gravity, he discovered that the earth's crust below the oceans is thinner than under the continents.

By dating the uppermost layers of sediment in sample cores with the radiocarbon method and calculating the rate of sediment accumulation, Ewing was also able to predict that the ocean floor is much younger than the 4.5-billion-year age of the earth. The oldest sediment ever recovered by deep-sea drilling is 170 million years old.[6]

Ocean soundings also revealed another puzzling characteristic of the seafloor. Ocean sediments were unbelievably thin. "It dawned on us near the end of the fifties," says David Ericson, who wrote about the sediments with Ewing and others. "Something must have happened about a hundred million years ago to renew or drastically reorganize the earth's crust under the oceans."[7]

Scientists began taking a second look at a theory by Alfred Wegener. In 1920 this meteorologist proposed that millions of years ago there was just one large landmass. It cracked, he said, and the continents then drifted apart. The records that Ewing and others were gathering tied in with a number of updated theories. Two American geologists, Harry

The Mid-Atlantic Ridge is a chain of undersea mountains that lies between North and South America in the west and Europe and Africa in the east. Ewing studied this ridge extensively and made many new discoveries about its origins and composition.

Hess and Robert Dietz, proposed the theory of seafloor spreading. Millions of years ago, they said, the crust of the earth underneath the midocean ridge cracked and was pulled apart. As lava oozed up into the crack from the molten layer underneath the crust, it solidified and forced the ocean floor to spread. Scientists now support a theory called plate tectonics. According to this theory, the earth's crust is made up of huge, thick plates. When the plates collide, mountains are thrust up—such as the Himalayas. Where plates slide past each other, there is an earthquake fault—such as the San Andreas Fault in California. Today's scientists agree that the earth's crust is always subject to change and there is much to learn about the ocean bottom, particularly its ridges and valleys.

Much of what we know about the ocean bottom, however, we owe to Maurice Ewing's pioneering research. He was a founding member of the Joint Oceanographic Institutions for Deep Earth Sampling (JOIDES). Its goal is to define the earth's history by sampling the sediment of the ocean floor. Today, JOIDES continues its mission by drilling into rocks beneath the seafloor to determine how and when they were formed and changed. It also researches other projects, such as world climate change.

Divorced a second time in 1965, Ewing married Harriet Bassett the same year. In 1972 Ewing retired as a professor at Columbia and director of its

Lamont-Doherty observatory. He returned to his home state, taking a position at the University of Texas at Galveston. There, with a group of colleagues, he formed the Earth and Planetary Sciences Division of the Marine Biomedical Institute. He established a well-recognized center of lunar and earthquake seismology. He died in 1974, but he left a legacy of scientific investigations that other scientists pursue today. He was honored with numerous scientific awards and eleven honorary doctorates. The Lamont-Doherty observatory honored Ewing by naming a research ship after him. As his colleague Sir Edward Bullard pointed out, Ewing's first achievement was to show that geologists could do a range of things in the ocean that no one had thought of doing before. He knew what he wanted to do, he found ways of doing it, and he persuaded other people to help him.[8]

Ernest Everett Just

2

Ernest Everett Just
Understanding the Cell

From the tiniest sand dollar on a beach to the largest whale, every living thing begins growing as an embryo. Biologist Ernest Everett Just contributed much to our knowledge in this area. He was one of the first African-American scientists to be recognized professionally for his work. His first book, *The Biology of the Cell Surface*, was published in 1939. It was the result of research he conducted at the Marine Biological Laboratory in Woods Hole, Massachusetts, in the 1920s and in Europe in the 1930s.

Ernest Everett Just was born August 14, 1883, in Charleston, South Carolina. His father was a construction worker on the Charleston docks. His mother was a seamstress.

When Ernest was four years old, both his father and grandfather, who had helped support the family, died. His mother then became a teacher in a small elementary school. In the summers she worked at a phosphate mine on nearby James Island. On the island she saw vacant land that could be made into small farms at low cost. So she persuaded a group of African-American families to move from Charleston to the island. There they founded a new town, which was called Maryville in her honor. Maryville was the first town in South Carolina to be governed entirely by African Americans.

Mary Just wanted her son Ernest to follow her example and become a teacher. She sent him to an all-African-American boarding school in Orangeburg, South Carolina, when he was thirteen. The school taught trade skills such as carpentry and bricklaying to boys, but it also prepared young people to teach in all-African-American grade schools. Ernest completed his teacher preparation studies at this school in just three years and then sought higher educational opportunities. His mother had read that the Kimball Union Academy in New Hampshire offered scholarships to exceptional students. Ernest applied and was awarded a scholarship, but his family had no transportation money to give him. So Ernest worked his way to New York aboard a ship. His total pay for the trip was only five dollars. Once in New York, he took a job as a cook to earn enough money for a train ticket to New Hampshire. He completed Kimball's four-year program in three years. He graduated in 1903 with the highest grades in his class. But his mother did not get to see him graduate; she died during his second year at the academy.[1]

After Kimball, Just attended Dartmouth College. He supported himself with scholarships and an occasional loan. He looked forward to intellectual companionship and hoped that college would offer him a scholar's life. But he had not been on the campus a week before he felt keen disappointment. Men at the college talked with excitement about only one topic—football. Dartmouth had just beaten rival Harvard University. But Just wasn't interested in the game. Other students considered him a traitor because he didn't root for the team.

By the middle of his sophomore year, Just was about ready to quit. Then, in his first course in biology, he read an essay on the development of the egg. (The egg cell is particularly interesting because out of it comes the complex development found in multicellular organisms, including human beings.) From that time on, the cell became the focus of his study. Cells are studied by all biologists, but the egg cell and its development is the special interest of scientists called embryologists. Just took all of the college's courses in biology and zoology. He graduated in 1907 magna cum laude (a Latin phrase meaning "with great praise" and representing a college degree awarded with high honor). He was the only member of his class with that honor.[2]

That same year Just was offered a teaching position at Howard University in Washington, D.C. Initially a teacher of English and rhetoric, his salary was four hundred dollars per year. With his interest in science, Just was encouraged to consider medicine. But research in biology was the career he wanted. He consulted his former biology teacher at Dartmouth, William Patten. Patten put him in touch with Frank R. Lillie, chairman of the Department of Zoology at the University of Chicago. Lillie was also director of the Marine Biological Laboratory, the premier institution for the study of how marine animals develop and live. Just went to work as a lab assistant with Lillie in Woods Hole in the summer of 1909.

Just continued teaching English at Howard during the regular school terms, adding biology courses to his schedule. Later, he was appointed a professor of biology. At the same time, he was also a professor of physiology in the medical school. He was then making a salary of $2,150 per year and was influential in science education at Howard University.[3] His teaching methods and his creative approaches to laboratory techniques and the design of experiments motivated students.

At Woods Hole, Just displayed the intelligence, imagination, and unending patience needed for research. During this period, Just was also taking graduate courses in zoology and embryology. He published his first scientific paper in the *Biological Bulletin* in 1912. It was the first of many papers about cells and the fertilization of the eggs that develop into the marine life we find in the ocean. Just had embarked on his life's work.[4]

In the 1920s, when Just started researching, most biologists thought that the nucleus was the most important part of the cell. Since it contains the DNA (deoxyribonucleic acid), which directs the making of duplicate cells, biologists thought that the nucleus controlled *all* of the activities of the cell. They thought that the cytoplasm surrounding the nucleus was unimportant, and hardly anyone ever mentioned the ectoplasm, the outer surface of the cytoplasm. Just began to see that the ectoplasm was just as important as the nucleus in embryonic development. There are factors in the cytoplasm and ectoplasm that are necessary to tell the nucleus what to do, he found. They take an active role in how the organism develops. Just's research in marine organisms helped later scientists reach additional conclusions. As a result of Just's work, medical scientists also began to research the work of cells in the human liver, kidneys, and other vital organs. They took a new look at the relationship between the cell and its surrounding ectoplasm.[5]

In 1915 Just was awarded the first Spingarn Medal by the National Association for the Advancement of Colored People in New York. This annual award is presented "to the man or woman of African descent and American citizenship who shall have made the highest achievement in the previous year."[6] The recognition encouraged him to pursue his research despite the obstacles he faced in a segregated society.

At the time of this award, Just had not yet earned his doctorate. Lillie arranged for him to enter the doctoral program at the University of Chicago. Just's teaching duties at Howard delayed his completion of a dissertation, but his Ph.D. was awarded in 1916.[7]

Just spent twenty summers at Woods Hole. As Lillie wrote of Just in *Science*, "He became more widely acquainted with the embryological resources of the marine fauna than probably any other person."[8] In 1922 Just was invited to give a series of lectures at the Marine Biological Laboratory. By this time he had published nearly twenty scientific papers. The most notable of these were a series of articles examining the fertilization reaction—what happens when sperm reaches the surface of the egg— in a species of sand dollar. Previous work in this area had been done by Lillie and biologist Jacques Loeb. The articles, based on solid research, spelled out Just's explanation of some basic questions about the interaction of sperm and egg.

During the 1920s other African-American scientists began to spend summers in Woods Hole. They were accepted at the laboratory as professional equals. However, Just's attempt to bring his wife and family there in 1927 proved disastrous. Openly shunned by some of the white wives in the community,

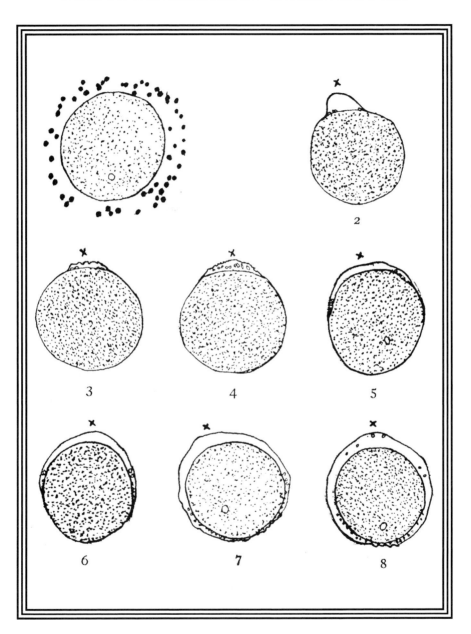

Just studied and sketched out the different stages of egg fertilization
in the sand dollar.

who were not willing to accept African Americans socially, Ethel Just returned to Washington with her children. At the same time, Just was growing impatient at the laboratory. Constantly sought out by others for help because of his acknowledged authority on the preparation and handling of marine eggs, he was kept from his own research by the interruptions.

In 1929 he received an invitation to work at the Stazione Zoologica in Naples, Italy. He began a decade of biological research in Europe, earning fellowships and foundation grants while on leave from teaching. He was welcomed at the Sorbonne in Paris. The Kaiser Wilhelm Institute for Biology in Berlin offered him research opportunities, as did another research institute in Brittany. Meanwhile, despite poor health with an intestinal illness, he continued teaching at Howard when not in Europe.[9]

While in Germany, Just fell in love with a young woman named Hedwig Schnetzler. He lived with her for eight years while he was conducting research in Europe. Just asked his wife for a divorce, but she initially refused. In 1938 Just permanently moved to France, and he began to think of that country as his home. He obtained a European divorce and married Hedwig in 1939.[10] Disaster struck in 1940 when the Germans invaded France. The research lab where Just worked was ordered to close its facilities to foreigners, and Just was imprisoned for a short time. Since the United States was not yet involved in the war, State Department officials were able to free him. But his intestinal illness had worsened in prison. He returned to America with Hedwig and made an attempt to resume teaching at Howard. He considered resuming his research at Woods Hole, but on October 27, 1941, he died of stomach cancer.[11]

Ernest Everett Just published seventy-five scientific papers in addition to two books. For Just, the cell surface held an almost spiritual fascination. Here were fundamental processes of life. Here, too, were answers to the mysteries of heredity and evolution—the characteristics we inherit from our parents and our ancestors. His studies served as a guide for future scientists of embryology.[12] He overcame economic hardship and racial prejudice to become a leader in his scientific field. The United States belatedly recognized his achievements on February 1, 1996, by issuing a postage stamp in his honor.

Sylvia A. Earle

3

Sylvia A. Earle

Exploring and Explaining Marine Life

"Suppose the oceans dried up tomorrow. Why should I care? I don't swim. I hate boats. I get seasick. I don't even like to eat fish. Who needs the oceans?" Those questions, posed by a mischievous Australian interviewer to marine biologist Sylvia Earle in 1976, were mild, Earle says. "Over the years, I came into contact with many people who do not seem to know or care about the sea."[1]

Sylvia Earle is a tireless advocate for preserving a healthy ocean environment. Her work with government agencies and her lectures and writings for the general public accompany a forty-year career as a marine scientist. She is also a record-holding diver and explorer of the deep sea.

Earle was born August 30, 1935, in Gibbstown, New Jersey. Her father was an electrician, and her mother was a nurse. Earle's love of the ocean began when her family moved from New Jersey to the west coast of Florida. "I was shown fish and other creatures with a positive attitude, not 'yuk'," she says,

My mother would bring frogs to my brothers and me. She would tell us how beautiful they are and how fascinating it was to look at their gorgeous golden eyes.[2]

When I was seventeen, I took a summer class in marine biology. My first scuba instruction consisted of two words: "Breathe naturally." I remember putting on the tank and the big double-hose regulator. My first dive was out in the open sea. It was in the Gulf of Mexico, 5 miles offshore. It was in the middle of a grass bed filled with so much action. There were little fish, starfish, sea urchins, crabs. Immediately scuba became a means to an end. Not an end in itself. It was glorious, and still is![3]

Earle graduated from high school at age sixteen. She earned her bachelor's degree from Florida State University at nineteen and her master's from Duke University at twenty. She then began work on the biology of algae for her doctorate. Algae is the name given to most of the plants that live in the ocean and in freshwater.

In 1957 Earle married Jack Taylor, a graduate student of zoology. While their two children were young, Earle took a job with the National Park Service. During the 1960s she collected samples and made thousands of records of marine algae on the Gulf of Mexico coastline. Her explorations also took her on five expeditions far from home.

Earle's first chance to view deep-sea life from a submarine came in 1968. She was participating as the only woman scientist in the Smithsonian-Link Man in the Sea program, exploring the waters of the Bahamas. Ed Link, developer of the program, described the *Deep Diver*'s operation this way: "We park her [the sub] on the bottom and build up the gas pressure in the divers' compartment until it equals the pressure on the outside; the hatch drops open and out they go."[4] Earle had an hour and a half for her marine explorations—four times longer than usual at deep depths. Then she climbed back into the sub. The hatch was closed, decompression began, and she returned to the surface.

The goal of this program was to extend the length of time that divers could stay underwater at great depths, once an equilibrium had been reached between the pressure inside their bodies and the surrounding water. Earle saw how much technology could offer to marine scientists, who could use it to accomplish more on each dive.

How would you like to *live* underwater for two weeks? In 1970 Sylvia Earle led a team of women scientists in the Tektite II project. This was an underwater living experiment sponsored by several government agencies. Space scientists thought that what was learned about living underwater would be helpful to astronauts in weightless space. Fish and plant scientists watched the experiment because they wanted to develop a system to study marine life for sustained periods.

One development of the experiment was a new rebreathing system for use underwater. In the rebreathing system, air exhaled by the diver passes through a filter carried in a backpack. The filter chemically removes the carbon dioxide so the clean air can be rebreathed by the diver. No bubbles are released from this system. To Earle, that meant more freedom to explore marine life. She could see and hear more as a silent human "fish" than she could wearing a noisy, bubbly scuba, and she could stay underwater longer.[5]

The team of women scientists drew a lot of attention from the media, which dubbed them the "aquababes." The media exposure helped Earle see another important role she could play. Through books, lectures, and television documentaries, she could help the public understand and respect the ocean and its occupants.

Earle set her first deep-dive record in 1979, diving to 1,250 feet. She showed that a diver could go deep, do a job, and return without having to spend time in a decompression chamber. Previously, a diver who had been working under the intense atmospheric pressure in the deep ocean had to enter the chamber, which gradually let his or her body readjust to surface atmospheric pressure.

The metal Jim suit (named after Jim Jarrett, the diver who was first to test it) made decompression unnecessary. At 1,250 feet below sea level, the pressure on the Jim suit is 600 pounds per square inch. (On land we experience atmospheric pressure of only 14.7 pounds per square inch of our body.) If there had been a leak in the suit, Earle might have been crushed to death.

The suit is usually occupied by a 200-pound man, but it was reconfigured for Earle's shorter, 110-pound body. Wearing this Jim suit, Earle was carried down to the ocean floor on a small submarine, the *Star II*. It was fitted with a platform on which she could stand during descent. When she left the platform on the bottom, only a thin communication cable connected her to the *Star II*.

But as Earle spent two and a half hours exploring the ocean bottom, her thoughts were not of danger but of what she was discovering: marine life no one had ever seen before. The seafloor's slopes and ridges teem with life.

> Bright red galatheid crabs swaying on the branches of a pink sea fan; a small, sleek, dark brown lantern fish darting by with lights glistening along its sides. I could see sparks of living light, blue-green flashes of small transparent creatures brushed against my faceplate.[6]

Earle is a record-holding deep-sea diver as well as a marine biologist and environmentalist.

The experience made Earle want to dive even deeper in the ocean but in a dream machine with gathering devices that were more like human arms and hands. To that end she cofounded, with British engineer Graham Hawkes, a manufacturing company called Deep Ocean Engineering. They built the *Deep Rover*, a submersible used by Earle and other scientific researchers, and the *Phantom*, a small remotely operated vehicle (ROV). In 1993, a scientist working in California remotely operated a *Phantom* underneath the ice of Antarctica.[7]

Earle left Deep Ocean Engineering in 1990 to accept an appointment from the president of the United States as chief scientist of the National Oceanic and Atmospheric Administration (NOAA). She was the first woman to hold that position. As indicated by its name, NOAA researches and monitors the oceans and the atmosphere. It protects marine resources, forecasts weather, and monitors pollution.

While at NOAA, Earle saw the devastation to ocean life in the Persian Gulf caused by oil spills during the 1991 Gulf War. Before Iraq's army was driven out of Kuwait, which it had invaded, it set afire seven hundred oil wells. As a result, 500 million gallons of oil pollution flowed into the coastal waters of the Persian Gulf.

Back in Washington, Earle saw the difficulties in achieving her environmental goals within the framework of her position. Scientists who want to preserve ocean life are frequently in conflict with fishing interests, navies, and others who want free access to all parts of the sea. In January 1992 she announced her resignation. "As private citizen Earle," she said, "I will be able to actively seek, not just to advocate, a healthy and sustainable marine environment."[8]

In 1992 Earle founded Deep Ocean Exploration and Research. It provides support services and technical expertise in the use of ROVs and submersibles. Its clients include scientists and other underwater professionals.

In 1998 she was named explorer in residence by the National Geographic Society. Earle envisions a future when technological improvements will allow even deeper ocean research.

Earle has led more than fifty expeditions worldwide. She has spent more than six thousand hours underwater in connection with her scientific research. Earle continues to travel to Washington and other cities to plead for a "sea change" in our attitude about the ocean. She is often asked what is the greatest threat to the oceans.

> If I had to name the single most dangerous threat . . . it's the base of all the others: ignorance. A failure to make the connection between the health of coral reefs and our own health. Between the fate of the great whales and the future of mankind. With knowing comes caring. With caring, there is hope that we will find harmony with the natural systems that sustain us.[9]

Her more than one hundred publications further marine science and technology. But her general interest lectures—in sixty countries—alert public awareness to ocean concerns. Her television programs, such as the *National Geographic Explorer*, reach millions more. Will these and the efforts of other scientists keep the oceans safe for the future of our planet?

Roger Revelle

Roger Revelle

Grandfather of the Greenhouse Effect

Is the earth heating up? Today's scientists still ask the question that Roger Revelle posed forty years ago.

In 1957, Revelle published a paper with colleague Hans Suess. They were concerned about the burning of fossil fuels such as coal and oil, which release carbon dioxide into the atmosphere. Revelle said,

> I knew about the buffer mechanism of seawater [the capacity of the ocean to absorb carbon dioxide], a result of the relationship of carbonate, bicarbonate and carbon ions. This meant that we could have a considerable increase, even by a factor of ten, of carbon dioxide in the atmosphere without much change in oceanic carbon dioxide. Though there is fifty times as much carbon dioxide in the oceans than in the atmosphere, it's

very hard to get more carbon dioxide into the ocean.[1]

That means most of it goes into the atmosphere. There the increased carbon dioxide traps more of the sun's heat—just as it does in a plant greenhouse— warming the earth.

Revelle decided to set up a laboratory to monitor carbon dioxide levels in the atmosphere over a long period. He recruited Dr. Charles Keeling to head the Carbon Dioxide Research Group at the Scripps Institution of Oceanography in 1956. Keeling's measurements, which are still being gathered yearly, are one of the most important sources of data for studying the greenhouse effect. Revelle also got other international scientists to cooperate in gathering data.

Why should anyone care about a few degrees in temperature? Because too much heat could melt polar ice. Ocean levels would rise, and coastal states would become flooded with the rising seawater. Marine organisms would have to move to cooler waters. Agriculture could also be affected if the earth heated up too much, causing droughts.

As scientists monitor carbon dioxide, they alert the public to other greenhouse gases such as methane (a natural gas formed by the decay of plant and animal matter) and nitrous oxide (used in making pressurized canned foods such as instant whipped cream). There are things we can do to reduce or eliminate greenhouse gases. Making sure we have enough trees, which use carbon dioxide, is just one idea. Substituting solar energy or ocean thermal energy for energy from coal, oil, and natural gas is another. More study about the role of the oceans in the changes of oceanic and atmospheric climate will be important. "Research and observations over the next 10 to 20 years should give us a much better idea of the likely magnitude of . . . warming," Revelle wrote in 1992.[2]

Born in Seattle on March 7, 1909, Revelle was schooled at home until he was eight years old. The family then moved to southern California, hoping the warmer climate would be better for his mother's asthma.

Like many other oceanographers, Revelle initially had a different career in mind. When he entered Pomona College in 1925 at the age of sixteen, he hoped to become a journalist. He liked writing, and he was editor of both his high school newspaper and the college humor magazine.

It was his college geology teacher, Alfred O. Woodford, however, who opened Revelle's eyes to the wonders of science. On their first field trip, Woodford assembled the class near the campus and asked, "How did this hill get here? Look around and tell me what you see and think." Geologists study the origin, history, and structure of the earth. They want to know how hills were formed and where the oceans came from. So did Revelle.

Revelle said Woodford taught him three vital lessons: Learn the vocabulary of geology, "so that I was able to read the literature easily;" little was known about the earth, but research could find out a great deal; and geological research was exciting and fun.[3]

After graduating from Pomona with a degree in geology in 1929, Revelle spent a year there working with Woodford. His fiancée, Ellen Virginia Clark, was a junior at nearby Scripps College. Ellen was the great-niece and namesake of the philanthropist Ellen Browning Scripps.

In 1931 Revelle became a teaching assistant in geology at the University of California at Berkeley. The director of the Scripps Institution of Oceanography visited Berkeley seeking a graduate student. He needed a researcher to spend a year classifying deep-sea mud samples from the Atlantic and Pacific oceans. Since Scripps was located in La Jolla, the hometown of his fiancée, Revelle applied and was hired.

In a paper published in 1987, Revelle described "How I Became an Oceanographer and Other Sea Stories." He worked in the laboratory at Scripps along with four other research assistants. One day a colleague came to the lab and said, "You're the new boy here. Tomorrow we go to sea. I'll pick you up in front of your house at 2:30 A.M." That first shipboard experience started in pitch darkness in the ocean off the coast of San Diego. Taking mud samples all day, returning well after dark, was "one of the finest days I had ever spent. I believe I decided then and there . . . that I would spend the rest of my life as an oceanographer. Being at the same time a sailor and a scientist seemed too good to be true."[4] Revelle had found a way to pursue geology without climbing mountains, which he dreaded because of acrophobia (intense fear of high places). And the oceans offered exciting prospects for scientific discovery.

That was the beginning of a science career exploring the seafloor with geophysical instruments. Even those mud samples, his earliest job, fit in with his lifelong interest in calcium carbonate and carbon dioxide. Through them, Revelle became interested in the buffer mechanism of seawater. When carbon dioxide dissolves in seawater, it sets up a series of chemical reactions. These act as a buffer to prevent sudden changes in the acidity or alkalinity of the seawater.

Eventually, Revelle realized that the oceans were not absorbing as much carbon dioxide as earlier scientists had assumed. This meant that the rest of the carbon dioxide created by the burning of fossil fuels was going into the atmosphere. These facts led to his concerns about global warming. And with his work with mud samples, Revelle also earned a doctorate from the University of California.

In 1936 Revelle was assigned by Scripps to a Navy submarine tender to make oceanographic measurements. The navy's entire submarine fleet of six subs and two tenders participated in the training cruise.

Revelle began to see how the science of oceanography could be very important to the navy and its operations, so he joined the naval reserve.

In the summer of 1936, Revelle also accepted an invitation to spend a year of study at the Geophysical Institute in Bergen, Norway. Enroute to Europe, Revelle stopped over in Washington. He wanted to gauge navy interest in possible joint research with Scripps. The Navy was formulating arguments to use to secure funding for ships. And Revelle wanted to be sure that the Navy would be calling on Scripps for research. Revelle proposed that Scripps's study of changes in oceanic circulation could have possible applications for long-range weather forecasting for the navy. He also suggested that the Scripps Institution's investigations of physical and chemical oceanography could aid fisheries and allied industries. In addition, Revelle said that oceanic research could help geologists understand marine sedimentation in their search for petroleum.

Before arriving in Norway, Revelle also attended an international conference in Edinburgh. He presented several papers written with Scripps colleagues. They included a significant finding on the distribution of oxygen and phosphate in the North Pacific Ocean. In 1936, oceanography was so new that the group of thirty oceanographers attending that meeting included most of the world's leading ocean experts at that time.[5]

Revelle returned to Scripps after his year in Norway. His first expeditions for Scripps were to the Gulf of California. No hydrographic survey (charting of the waters and underwater features) had ever been made of this area between the Baja peninsula and Mexico. Discoveries of steep ridges and deep basins puzzled the explorers. Later scientists recognized that aspects of the gulf's geology were similar to other sea bottoms where a boundary between tectonic plates exists.

In July 1941 Revelle was called to active duty in the Navy. He rose through the ranks from sonar officer to head of the geophysics branch of the Office of Naval Research. After World War II ended, he became responsible for the oceanographic aspects of the atomic bomb tests in the western Pacific Ocean. Global warfare had made an understanding of oceanography essential to national security.

In 1950 Revelle became acting director of Scripps. That summer he led the Scripps Institution's and the Navy Electronics Laboratory's joint Mid-Pacific Expedition (Mid-Pac). It was a three-month, twenty-five-thousand-mile voyage. Mid-Pac explored the structure and thickness of the crust of the earth beneath the Pacific. The expedition drew the first continuous profile of the seafloor. (Depth recordings could be taken continuously from a moving ship so that a chart of bottom depths could be drawn on paper.) On September 9, 1950, Revelle made headlines around the world when he discovered an

Revelle (right) removes a sample core of the sea bottom during an early expedition.

undersea mountain range with peaks almost fourteen thousand feet tall.

Revelle continued to lure leading physicists, chemists, and biologists to Scripps. His goal was to create a great technical oceanographic research and teaching institution. Under his direction, Scripps researchers were important in the development of the theories of seafloor spreading and plate tectonics.[6]

In 1961 Revelle took a two-year leave of absence to become science adviser to Secretary of the Interior Stewart Udall. While in that position, Revelle's interest in the worldwide problems affecting society increased. He spent the next ten years as director of the Harvard University Center for Population Studies, and he was deeply involved in many aspects of the United Nations Educational, Scientific, and Cultural Organization (UNESCO).[7]

Revelle published more than two hundred papers and received many awards related to his work. In 1975 Revelle retired from Harvard and returned to the University of California, San Diego, as professor of science and public policy. He and his wife, Ellen, were active in community affairs. They had three daughters and one son. But Revelle never retired from his interest in the ocean and its effect on the world. He was the first chairman of the International Committee on Climatic Changes and the Ocean, which encouraged countries to cooperate and share information on large climate studies. Revelle was also an active participant in the National Academy of

Sciences, an honorary organization of outstanding American scientists.

Roger Revelle died July 15, 1991. He was active in global issues to the end. Scripps Institution of Oceanography named one of its newest research vessels in his honor.

Walter Munk

Measuring Ocean Climate Worldwide

Scientists know more today about global warming, wave action, tides, and the wobble of the earth's axis during rotation because of the work of Walter Munk. Born in 1917, Munk has spent nearly sixty years studying the ocean. But as he admits,

> I was an unlikely person for a career in oceanography. I grew up in Austria being interested only in skiing and tennis. My maternal grandfather was a banker in Vienna and I was supposed to follow him. In 1932 at the age of fourteen, I was sent to a boys' preparatory school in America to finish high school. I was then to be apprenticed to a financial firm in New York my grandfather had helped to found.[1]

Walter Munk

Munk spent three years at the bank but found it boring. He took some extension courses at Columbia University to continue his education. In 1937 he moved to California to study applied physics at the California Institute of Technology. After graduating in 1939—the same year he became a United States citizen—Munk applied for a summer job at the Scripps Institution of Oceanography. "After that first summer," says Munk, "I went back to Cal Tech for a master's degree in geophysics. But next summer I was back at Scripps requesting to be admitted for a Ph.D. degree in Oceanography." Harald Sverdrup, the Norwegian Arctic explorer, was then director of Scripps. He warned Munk that he could not think of a single job in oceanography that would be available in the next ten years. Munk went ahead anyway and became, for a while, the only student at Scripps. Today, Scripps, which is part of the University of California, has a student body of more than one hundred and fifty.

In 1938, when Germany annexed Austria just before the start of World War II, Munk enlisted in the United States Army. He served in the field artillery and the ski battalion. But then he was given the opportunity to join a small oceanographic group at the Navy's Radio and Sound Laboratory at Point Loma, California. A week later Japan attacked Pearl Harbor, and the United States entered World War II. For the next six years, Munk worked on problems of amphibious warfare for the Navy.

An example of one of these wartime problems concerned ocean waves. As Munk recalls,

> In 1942, we were told of preparations for an amphibious winter landing on the northwest coast of Africa. The coast is subject to a heavy northwesterly swell [large waves]. When these waves break on shore, they exceed six feet on two out of three days in winter. The problem was to pick the one day out of three when the waves are suitable for landing.[2]

Munk and Sverdrup worked on the problem together. They studied weather maps. They observed the waves caused by wind over oceans, lakes, and laboratory wave tanks. They created a mathematical formula of wave prediction based on three factors. The height and time period of storm-generated waves, they found, are related to the speed of the wind, the storm fetch (how far the wind is reaching), and how long the storm lasts.

Their method of predicting the correct timing for a landing was successful. It was taught to Navy and Air Force weather officers, who applied it in both the Pacific and Atlantic theaters of World War II. A peacetime adaptation of this science enabled oil companies drilling in the oceans to protect their rigs from the force of waves.

Munk is perhaps best known for his ongoing work in ocean acoustic thermometry (measuring ocean temperature with sound waves). Scientists are concerned about whether the earth's atmosphere is gradually warming and whether the polar ice caps will melt. Their question was, How can we determine the temperature of the water around the entire world on a continuous basis? Walter Munk came up with the answer. Scientists have known for some time that sound travels almost five times faster through water than through air. They also know that it travels faster in warm water than it does in cold water.

In 1960 scientists had experimented with transmitting sound from explosives off the coast of Australia. The sound was picked up by receivers in the waters off Bermuda—halfway around the world—3.7 hours later.[3] Munk was intrigued with the result.

But could this experiment be enlarged? Could scientists use the numerous existing Navy listening posts to measure sound transmissions through various areas of the ocean and arrive at accurate water temperatures? Munk proposed conducting experiments at Heard Island. Why Heard Island? Because, says Munk, "its location in the Southern Indian Ocean is 'in view' along great circle routes with all major ocean basins. We were intrigued by the circumstance that the Heard Island sound source would be heard on both sides of North America."[4]

Some scientists worry that the loud sounds created by the experiments may harm marine mammals. "Certainly whales can hear for many tens of miles," says Munk, "and it's a legitimate concern."[5]

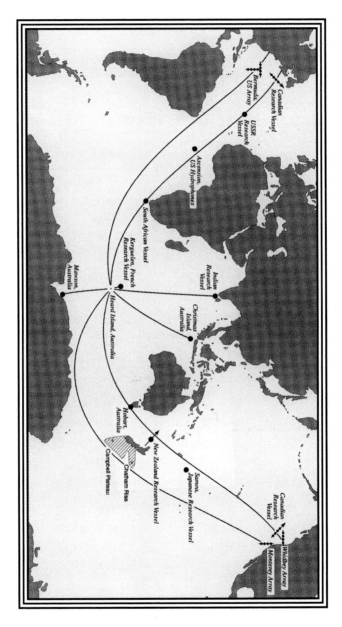

This map shows the names and locations of the various listening posts used during Munk's Heard Island Experiment.

In response, part of the ongoing study also monitors the behavior of sea creatures.

"The underlying thread to my work," says Munk, "is to collect lengthy studies of ocean waves, tides, temperatures and other factors. Then by using high-speed computers to help us analyze the data we gather, we have been able to formulate some ideas useful to oceanographers."[6] For example, one of the techniques Munk uses is called spectral analysis. Just as we see different frequencies of light waves as a spectrum of different colors—as in a rainbow—we can see a spectrum of frequencies in ocean waves. Low frequencies (long periods of time) are associated with swells, and high frequencies (short periods of time) are associated with wind-chopped waves. If you're at an ocean beach, you may notice low-frequency waves coming in at around four waves a minute; later that same day, high-frequency wind-chopped waves may come in at ten to twenty waves a minute. A swell might be compared to infrared light waves and a chop to ultraviolet light waves. Scientists can then measure how much energy is represented by each of the frequency bands in the wave spectrum. Commercial users of this kind of spectral analysis include companies that help ships plot their routes—not always by the shortest route but by avoiding the worst waves.[7]

Until 1982 Munk served as director of the La Jolla Laboratory of the Institute of Geophysics and Planetary Physics at the University of California.

The institute studies the earth, its interior, and its atmosphere and oceans, using methods of experimental and mathematical physics.

Munk has written more than two hundred scientific papers on his oceanographic discoveries. He has earned numerous scientific awards in Europe as well as in the United States. His book *Ocean Acoustic Tomography* was published by Cambridge University Press in 1995. In hospitals, a CAT scan uses X rays to map a part of the human body. At sea, scientists use computer-aided tomography with sound waves and other information to create a picture of the ocean. The oceanographer's job is complicated by the fact that the ocean is not a stationary solid object. It has currents and internal waves, and sound travels through it at varying speeds. Munk and his colleagues used a series of buoys that could both send and receive underwater sound. They created a three-dimensional map of the water temperature and the velocity of the current in the area crisscrossed by their instruments.

On Munk's sixty-fifth birthday, October 19, 1982, his colleagues surprised him with a celebration. To honor his accomplishments, they held a symposium on oceanography. The papers the scientists presented that day on internal ocean waves, tides, sound transmission, earth rotation, and styles of spectral analysis represented developments of ideas and studies pioneered by Munk.

Walter Munk and his sculptor wife, Judith, have two grown daughters who were born in 1956 and 1959. Munk says, "Neither of our daughters are scientists (although my younger daughter married a chemist) nor did I make any effort to steer them in that direction. The girls have minds of their own; but I take pride that they are also good skiers!"[8]

Eugenie Clark

6

Eugenie Clark

"The Shark Lady"

Scientists call Eugenie Clark an ichthyologist because she studies fish. Other people call her "the shark lady" because of her numerous articles and films on those ocean creatures. She has studied sharks in a laboratory, but she has also dived into the ocean to study them in their natural habitat. In the course of her studies, she has discovered new species.

What would you do if you were face-to-face with the largest fish in the world? Here's what Eugenie Clark did:

As I swim toward it, the whale shark alters course slightly to go deeper. This is typical evasive behavior when divers approach. Swimming as fast as I can, I can *just* keep up, but not for long. My hand trails down the massive body, over the thick, hard, textured skin. The shark feels like a wooden submarine. To stay with it longer, I propel myself up towards its dorsal fin. I find a handhold under the fin where it joins the body.

Feeling my touch, the shark speeds up. It is as though I am being towed through the water by a bus. I dare not look behind, for fear of having my face mask ripped away. Releasing my grip, I watch the vast, spotted creature sink slowly into the depths.[1]

This dive was one of the many Eugenie Clark made to learn more about this rare species of shark. The whale shark is about thirty feet long and weighs about twenty tons. If your calculator is handy, you'll discover that's forty thousand pounds of fish! No one knows how many whale sharks exist, where they live, or how deep they go. That's why Clark wanted to study them.

My interest in sharks started as a nine-year-old child in New York. My American father died when I was a baby. My Japanese-born mother was working at the newspaper stand in the lobby of the Downtown Athletic Club. On Saturdays while she worked, she left me nearby in the old New York Aquarium. I spent many hours watching the fishes.[2]

That was my first impression of these beautiful creatures—not like the introduction most kids have with a movie like *Jaws*. My feeling about sharks was to pretend I was in their world.[3]

Clark went to Hunter College in New York at age sixteen. She took comparative anatomy and started to learn shark anatomy. "I noticed two abdominal pores and asked the teacher what these pores did. She didn't know. Nobody knew. I thought I'd find out about these pores. I went on to do my Ph.D. work on freshwater fishes. My interest in sharks grew out of my more general interest in fishes."[4]

Eugenie Clark was born in New York on May 4, 1922. At Hunter College she majored in zoology. During the summers she took field courses at the University of Michigan Biological Station on Douglas Lake. After graduating in 1942, she married pilot Hideo "Roy" Imaki. Although she wanted a job related to her zoology background, the only job she could find during World War II was as a chemist at the Celanese Corporation of America. (Male chemists were in military service.) She earned her master's degree in 1946 and enrolled in New York University for her doctorate. Meanwhile, she worked evenings and weekends as a swimming instructor. That provided some part-time income, but swimming is also a valuable skill for a fish researcher!

In 1946 Clark was invited to join marine biologist Carl Hubbs at the Scripps Institution of Oceanography as his part-time research assistant. There Clark had her first exposure to a swell shark and her first walk on the bottom of the sea in a diving helmet. Diving became an important part of her research on all types of fish—whether with scuba equipment or in a deep diving submersible.

Back in New York, as she finished the last experiments for her dissertation, she was accepted for the Scientific Investigation in Micronesia program. This program supported field studies by six different scientists. One study involved poisonous fish. Clark had previously conducted research into puffers and trigger fish. That experience and her chemistry background were useful assets to the expedition. She also improved her skin-diving skills and learned spearfishing.[5]

In 1950 she read an article about the Red Sea Marine Biological Station. She applied for and won a Fulbright Scholarship to study poisonous fish in the Red Sea. The scholarship was part of an international exchange program of students and teachers named after United States senator William Fulbright, who introduced the legislation. "If I could dive in only one place in the world," Clark later wrote, "I would choose Ras Muhammad on the Red Sea."[6] Ras Muhammad is named for a huge rock on this peninsula that resembles the head of the prophet Muhammad. The variety and quantity of marine life there is what initially drew Clark to the area. It still does. She has made numerous diving expeditions to the Red Sea to expand her research on various types of fish.

With her excitement about her work and her ability to write for the general reader as well as for the scientific community, Clark has written many popular magazine articles. Her first book, *The Lady with a Spear*, was published in 1953. She then became an instructor in the biology department of Hunter College. She was also a research associate in animal behavior and ichthyology at the American Museum of Natural History in New York. Clark is still regularly invited to lecture at high schools, colleges, and universities.

One such invitation came from Anne and William H. Vanderbilt to give a lecture in Englewood, Florida. As a result, Clark was given the opportunity to start a laboratory of her own. Clark and her family moved to Florida. Clark's first marriage had ended after seven years. She was now married to her second husband, Ilias Papakonstantinou, an orthopedic physician, and they had two small children. After they moved from New York to Florida, Eugenie and Ilias had two more children. Clark's mother and stepfather followed the family to Florida and opened a Japanese restaurant nearby.

The Cape Haze Marine Laboratory became the site of Clark's marine research with sharks and other fish. These studies produced scientific papers on the reproductive methods of certain fish species, the use of shark livers in medical research, and shark learning and behavioral experiments. For example, Clark had proven with experiments that sharks can learn to press a target to obtain food. They could also be trained to tell the difference between targets of different shapes and colors.[7] As Clark's work with sharks and other fish became more well known, the lab received letters from students all over the country who wanted to work as volunteers with her during the summer. With National Science Foundation grants, Clark was able to work with some selected teachers and students on research projects both in the lab and in the Gulf of Mexico.

Scientific satisfactions were followed by personal grief. Clark's mother died from a brain hemorrhage (burst blood vessel) in 1959. "My stepfather had never mastered the English language. With no other Japanese people around, as there had been near his former restaurant in New York, he depended on my mother as his only close verbal companion."[8] Clark convinced her stepfather to move his restaurant closer to her home and to the new location of the marine laboratory on Siesta Key.

In 1965, Clark was invited to Japan as the guest of crown prince Akihito (now emperor), who, like his father, was interested in marine biology. Clark's scientific work with sharks had captured media attention, and her book had been translated and published in Japan. Her marriage, however, was providing other challenges. Clark's husband had become a successful investor, and his obsession with money was disturbing to Clark. She left her husband and they divorced. One of the many writers who had interviewed her over the years as she became well

Eugenie Clark is known as "the Shark Lady" because of her research on these fish.

known was Chandler Brossard. They married in 1967 and moved back to New York with Clark's four children.

Clark proposed Perry Gilbert as her successor at the marine laboratory. Gilbert was head of the Shark Research Panel of the American Institute of Biological Sciences. William Mote, a wealthy businessman, had consulted Clark earlier about expanding the marine laboratory. He acquired new land, and the newly named Mote Marine Laboratory opened with Perry Gilbert as its director.[9]

In 1968, Clark joined the zoology faculty at the University of Maryland. Along with her teaching she developed research programs in twenty other countries. Many of her major research discoveries were popularized in *National Geographic* magazine articles. In one, for example, she described "sleeping sharks" she studied in underwater caves in Mexico. Until this time, experts thought that sharks needed to swim nonstop in order to stay alive.[10] Clark's research papers covered not only sharks but also other fish like the Moses sole, garden eels, and tilefish. She discovered and described many new species. Some new species of fish (studied by others) have been named for her. Over the years Clark took all of her children on diving trips, and she even named one species, *Trichonotus nikii*, after her youngest child, Niki. It was a rare type of sand diver fish never previously reported in the Red Sea.

Clark's undersea expeditions progressed from the early ones with the heavy diving helmet to scuba diving then to seventy-one dives in deep-ocean submersibles. One dive, for example, in the *Pisces VI* submersible, resulted in a 1986 *National Geographic* article on deep-sea sharks. These sharks are among the least studied, but Clark pointed out, "You get more deep-sea creatures close to shore on a steep drop-off like Bermuda's [mid-Atlantic seamount] than on continental shelves."[11] Clark and her team were able to study and film deep-sea sharks and other rare fish in twelve-hour vigils in submersibles. Giant sharks were drawn in close to the submersible window by a small cage of cut-up fish bait.

Clark retired in 1992, but as professor emerita (honored for long service), she keeps her office and laboratory at the University of Maryland. She continues to teach and lead expeditions to many locations. She has worked on twenty-four television specials about marine life, and she has received numerous awards. In a 1996 interview before a lecture at the Houston Zoo, Clark mentioned that her four grown children could swim before they could walk. Her five-year-old grandson, Eli, was able to snorkel and dive and accompanied her on a Mexico trip in 1996 to look for whale sharks.[12]

In her lectures, Clark reminds her audience that most sharks do not bite people. Of the more than 370 species, most are harmless to humans. People do eat sharks and shark fin soup, though. Commercial fishing for sharks is depleting shark populations. As a result, in April 1997 the United States government started making laws to limit shark fishing.

Scientists like Eugenie Clark will continue to discover more about the ocean and its inhabitants. As a writer and a lecturer, she will also help us understand scientific discoveries.

7

Henry Stommel

Understanding Ocean Circulation and Atmosphere

Have you ever had intuition about something? A sudden thought that something must be true, even though you can not prove it? Henry Stommel had many such thoughts. He then discovered ways to prove them.

He was born September 27, 1920, in Wilmington, Delaware. His father was a chemist in the field of leather tanning. His mother, Marion Melson, was a very successful fund-raiser for large hospitals. Brought up in Freeport, on Long Island in New York, Henry spent much of his time sailing in small boats and tinkering with scientific gadgets, chemical experiments, microscopes, and aquatic bugs. The family later moved to Brooklyn, where Henry

Henry Stommel

attended public schools. He entered Yale at age eighteen.

An ocean scientist, Stommel started out looking up instead of down. He earned a bachelor of science degree in astronomy in 1942. He then attended Yale University Divinity School for half a year. He taught recruits at Yale and did research for the Navy in lieu of active duty during World War II.

Toward the end of World War II, Stommel became interested in the oceans and began teaching himself oceanography. He sometimes read as many as three books a day. In 1944 he became a research associate at the Woods Hole Oceanographic Institution. He published his first book in 1945, called *Science of the Seven Seas*. It describes the sea, the sky, and ocean life.[1] Stommel's book illustrates and explains waves and currents; winds and planets; whales and tiny creatures that glow in the deep dark sea.

During his early research, Stommel talked with Ray Montgomery, a colleague, about problems in oceanography. Montgomery mentioned how little was known about the dynamics of the Gulf Stream, the ocean current that flows northeast along the coast of North America.[2]

Spanish explorers knew about this "river" on the surface of the ocean as early as the 1500s. After their voyages to the New World, they rode its current back to Spain, but they kept their findings secret. It wasn't until Benjamin Franklin published a chart in 1770 that this current, which early American whalers had also observed, became widely known.[3]

Stommel wrote briefly about ocean currents in his first book. He described the influences of water temperature and density, prevailing winds, and the earth's rotation on the Gulf Stream. In 1948 he added another important observation. In a scientific paper, Stommel described the Gulf Stream's intensified speed along the United States's east coast. He presented the theory that similar currents should exist throughout the world's oceans along the boundaries of continents. This should be true regardless whether the current flows north or south, he said.[4] This paper is now one of the most frequently cited papers in modern oceanography.

In 1950 Stommel married Elizabeth Huntington Brown. They had two sons and a daughter. Stommel was an inventive father who made many toys for his children, including a one-passenger railroad system around his property. The rails were made of two-by-fours, and the engine was powered by a lawn-mower motor.[5]

In the 1950s Stommel observed that turbulence in the ocean caused warm water to flow downward. He assumed that colder water welled up from below to keep the temperature constant at any given level. Such circulation patterns had not been anticipated before. Scientists had long observed that the ocean's surface temperature remains fairly constant. If parts of the earth near the equator receive more heat from the sun than they are able to radiate and polar areas less, Stommel theorized, then the heated equatorial water and cold polar water must be circulating to maintain a heat balance.

This theory led to another theory. Stommel predicted that there was a southward flowing countercurrent *underneath* the Gulf Stream. This theory was confirmed in 1957. "It is one of the few purely theoretical predictions of a significant oceanic phenomenon," commented fellow scientist George Veronis.[6]

Scientists like Stommel were building on knowledge of the Coriolis effect, named after French mathematician Gaspard Coriolis. In 1835 Coriolis showed that the earth's rotation causes both winds and ocean currents to be deflected clockwise (to the right) in the Northern Hemisphere and counterclockwise (to the left) in the Southern Hemisphere. But Stommel added that currents exist not only on the surface but also at the sea bottom. We now have photographs of currents moving along the sea bottom. We also know that wastes deposited in certain areas of the ocean will be swept away by deep currents and deposited elsewhere.

Stommel's interest in the Gulf Stream expanded to study of other ocean currents—such as the Kuroshio off the coast of Japan—and to study of the physical composition of the ocean. During the 1960s Stommel helped establish international observation programs, including the Mid-Ocean Dynamics

Experiments. He also furthered interest in exploring the Indian Ocean. In the late 1970s, Stommel and colleagues studied currents in the northwestern Indian Ocean caused by monsoons (winds that change directions with the seasons). He also wanted to make data about the oceans more accessible. In 1963, he wrote a paper envisioning a computer that would produce graphs of different oceanographic variables on command. At that time, the approach was little more than a dream.[7]

In his book *A View of the Sea*, Stommel describes the cruises he made to the Azores, islands off the coast of Portugal. He wanted to study the shape of layers of dense water beneath the ocean's surface. By using an instrument called the CTD, Stommel measured the electrical conductivity, temperature, and depth of the water from the surface to the bottom at thirty different locations in a specific area. Why did he want this information? It would show him details about an ocean gyre in that part of the world. A gyre is a circular motion of water that exists in each of the major ocean basins. The water within each subtropical gyre turns clockwise in the Northern Hemisphere and counterclockwise in the Southern Hemisphere. In contrast, subpolar gyres in the Atlantic and Pacific have the opposite rotation—their direction depends on the winds.[8]

In 1981, the book *Evolution of Physical Oceanography* was published. It was a tribute to Stommel's immense contribution to the science. The

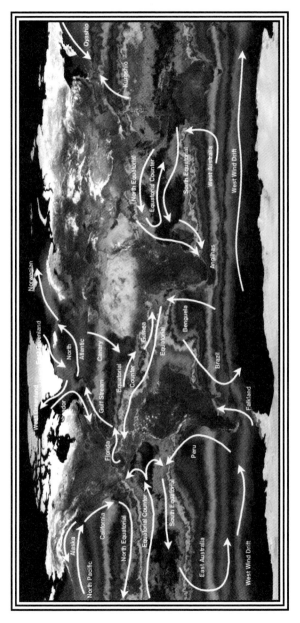

Stommel studied many of the ocean's currents, including the Gulf Stream off the east coast of the United States and the Kuroshio off the east coast of Japan.

editors pointed out Stommel's insistence on the importance of testing hypotheses.

In a 1989 speech before the Oceanography Society, Stommel offered words of encouragement to future ocean scientists: "Most theories are about observations that have already been made. It is therefore particularly exciting when a theorist comes up with an idea about a feature of the ocean that he is willing to go to sea for. I urge those entering the field to take the risk."

In that same talk, Stommel envisioned oceanography in the twenty-first century. Hundreds of remotely controlled robots will gather the undersea data that scientists need.[9] Gathering such data now, using a few ships in the huge ocean, is limiting; only a small amount of information can be gained in this way. Stommel's robots will get their power not from batteries but from the thermal energy of the ocean itself. A number of other scientists and engineers with similar ideas are currently at work on autonomous underwater vehicles.[10]

Stommel received numerous scientific awards in the United States and in foreign countries. The Royal Swedish Academy of Sciences, for example, acknowledged his "fundamental contributions . . . that in a unique way contributed to our understanding of the atmosphere and the sea."[11]

The joy Stommel felt in his chosen occupation was expressed when accepting one of his many awards. "The freedom to work full time in science . . .

unraveling some puzzle of nature is a privilege beyond compare."[12]

Henry Stommel continued to conduct research until he died in 1992. He applied mathematical models to the study of the oceans. He experimented in the earth's huge ocean laboratory. He made detailed observations and gave scientists further ideas to explore. He was an inspiration to generations of oceanographers and students throughout the world. He reminds us that oceanography is still a young science, and there is much we still don't know. It waits for the scientists of tomorrow to discover.

Allyn Vine

Allyn Vine

Pioneer of the Manned Deep-Sea Submersible

Oceanographers want to study the ocean. But they need equipment to help them discover its secrets. That's when a scientist like Allyn Vine comes in handy.

Today, oceanographers can explore the ocean floor in a tiny pressure-proof submarine. In the beginning, however, scientists thought this would be too risky. Not Allyn Vine, though. "We had about 45 oceanographic vessels around the world," he said. "That was like having a tool bag with 45 wrenches pretty much the same size. We wanted to see what a completely different wrench might be able to show us."[1]

Vine sought funding from the Office of Naval Research. First, many experiments had to be made to find the right materials. Which would hold up better under deep-sea pressure? What power source would work best? Many engineers worked with Allyn Vine on these problems. They used steel to form the prototype craft's hull. They used lead-acid golf-cart batteries to power the craft. For ballast (a heavy substance to improve stability), they designed a system using six hundred pounds of oil in six aluminum balls. The weight of the oil allowed the craft to dive. The oil could then be pumped into rubber-sided compartments to allow the sub to surface. When inflated with the oil, these membranes would increase the craft's displacement, pushing it up to the surface with about 350 pounds of force. A second ballast system—the same kind used on modern submarines—took in seawater to descend and discharged it to bring the sub back to the surface. Vine also designed a vital safety system: If the sub could not rise normally, everything would be dropped except the passenger sphere, which would rise to the surface.[2] Finally, in 1964, the first United States manned deep-sea submersible was christened. It was named *Alvin*—a contraction of <u>Al</u>lyn <u>Vine</u>— in his honor. This tiny research submarine has room for only three people: the pilot and two scientists. This seven-foot metal ball is no place for people who are claustrophobic.

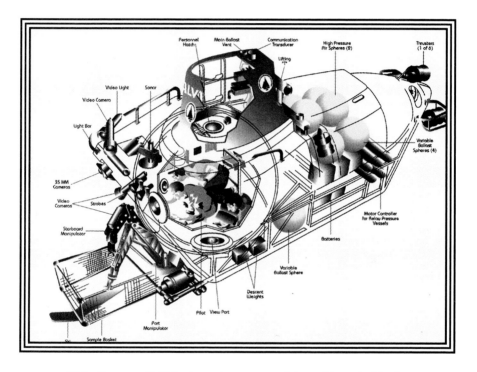

This diagram of *Alvin* shows how cramped it could get inside the deep-sea submersible.

Scientist and inventor Allyn Vine was born June 1, 1914, in Garrettsville, Ohio. His father was a butcher, and his mother was a housewife and antique dealer. He had three brothers. He loved school and experimenting. At the local telephone company junkyard, he'd look for wires and equipment to build things, such as burglar alarms.

He went to Hiram College, a small college just four miles from his home, where he majored in physics. This major turned out to be fruitful. He helped pay his way through college as a teaching assistant in the physics laboratories. He also met his future wife, Adelaide Holton, in the physics department.

After graduating from Hiram in 1936, Vine moved to Bethlehem, Pennsylvania, to get his master's at Lehigh University. His adviser was Maurice Ewing, one of the founders of modern oceanography. Ewing invited Vine to join him during the summers on the Woods Hole Oceanographic Institution's research vessel, the *Atlantis*. The vessel's mission was to conduct experiments to study the seafloor. After war broke out in Europe, the Navy began to fund major research projects at Woods Hole, and Vine became a salaried member of the institution. Along with Ewing, he developed the first remotely controlled camera to photograph the deep ocean floor.

One Navy project during the war attempted to improve detection of enemy submarines. Ewing's early experiments using explosives had shown how sound was transmitted through seawater. This experiment contributed to the invention of sonar (sound navigation and ranging), which helped the Navy find enemy submarines. By sending out a sound wave and then measuring the time it took the reflected sound to travel back, navy ships could tell how far away the target was. But some submarines seemed to be hiding beneath layers of low-density water, which deflected sonar beams.

One of the instruments ocean scientists use is the bathythermograph (BT). This instrument measures the temperature at different levels in the sea. It helped scientists find places where submarines might hide. Originally, seamen stopped a ship at a certain location, lowered a BT, took readings, and then moved on to the next location. Allyn Vine created a winch that could lower a BT from a moving ship and keep it at a constant depth. That gave scientists continuous readings over a broader area. Vine also increased the reliability and accuracy of the BT by adding a two-metal coil, with each metal having a different heat expansion rate. This compensated for the difference in temperature inside and outside the instrument.[3] The record of temperature and depth that Vine's device obtained was used to compute the paths of sound waves in the ocean. That revealed details of shadow zones and layers beneath which a submarine could hide.[4]

If improved BTs could help the navy find hiding enemy submarines, they might also help our subs avoid detection. Ewing and Vine designed a version of the BT to be used in submarines. This version showed American subs where a layer of low-density water was located so they could hide from their pursuers. Vine rode along in submarines and trained operators to use the BT to detect these layers. Vine's efforts brought a special commendation from the United States Navy. It honored him for "the saving of untold numbers of lives and millions of dollars of ships and equipment." His accomplishments also attracted funding from the Navy for the submersible *Alvin*.

Solving the construction problems of *Alvin* was one thing. The real test, however, came on July 20, 1964, when *Alvin* was to make its deepest dive—six thousand feet. It had been tested earlier in shallow waters, but now it was to be lowered into the deep ocean from its mother ship, *Lulu* (named after Vine's mother). On deck were Navy personnel; their approval was necessary for an official certification. On the previous test dive, the aft propeller had mysteriously stopped, and nobody knew why. *Alvin* was not unsafe without the prop, but it was less maneuverable.

The crew climbed into *Alvin* and submerged. At thirty-five hundred feet the aft propeller stopped. The sub continued descending. Three and a half hours after disappearing beneath the surface, *Alvin* touched bottom. The pilot cruised to investigate some marine life. When the fine clouds of sediment stirred up by *Alvin* settled, the creatures were gone. The pilot turned off *Alvin's* side propellers to see whether the creatures would come back. They didn't. Now, over the radio came, "*Alvin*, this is *Lulu*. It's time to start back up."

The pilot switched on the side propellers but nothing happened. He tried the aft propeller. Nothing. He threw the switch to pump oil into the ballast system. The pump groaned and *Alvin* began to rise. At fifty feet the pilot blew the seawater from the freeboard ballast tanks, and *Alvin* bobbed to the surface. Suddenly, all three propellers whirred on as *Alvin* cruised to the mother ship. The crew cheered. *Alvin* was certified.

But what had been the problem with the propellers? The dismantled *Alvin* had small granules of carbon gunking up its motors and electrical relays, produced when the electric parts came under the intense deep-sea pressure. In addition, the metal surrounding the aluminum propeller blades compressed during descent, touching the blades.[5]

Alvin has been continually redesigned and improved. Its personnel sphere is now made of titanium, and its onboard computers record and display the electronic data it gathers. How do scientists use *Alvin*? It helps oceanographers investigate the earth's structure under the sea, the ocean's chemistry, and marine life. Some of its special assignments make newspaper headlines. In 1966 the Navy used it to recover a hydrogen bomb that had fallen into the

Mediterranean Sea. In the 1970s researchers in it found hydrothermal vents and twelve-foot-long worms deep in the ocean, where little life was thought to exist. Others obtained information that confirmed the theory of seafloor spreading. In 1986 Robert Ballard used it to explore the "unsinkable" ocean liner *Titanic,* two miles down in the ocean. Much of Ballard's early research relied on *Alvin.* In 1994 *Alvin* celebrated its thirtieth birthday, having logged 2,772 dives for scientific research. It is currently rated to dive to 14,764 feet in the deep ocean. It continues to help geologists, physicists, marine biologists, and archeologists to explore the ocean bottom. Its special equipment includes cameras, rock drills, a mechanical arm, a magnetometer, a gravimeter, and other sophisticated recording devices.

Allyn Vine was the author or coauthor of sixty scientific papers and technical reports. He was involved in projects ranging from deep-sea geology and underwater acoustics to improving seagoing techniques for handling heavy gear. He designed special instruments to research potential uses of the oceans. Vine lobbied not only for the construction of his own projects but also for other tools like FLIP, the Floating Instrument Platform operated by the Scripps Institution of Oceanography. FLIP's 355-foot-long hull is towed to a research site. When its ballast tanks are flooded, the vessel "flips" upright to become a stable research vessel. It measures sound and energy waves at sea.

Scientists like Vine who are also innovative "tinkerers" tackle everyday problems, too. Once, Vine needed an early wake-up call but no alarm clock was available. The solution? He simply hooked his vacuum cleaner to the electric outlet on his stove and set the timer.[6]

Allyn Vine received numerous scientific awards. He realized the need to study the ocean for national defense, but he also saw the ocean as a common bond linking the nations of the world. To that end, he traveled and worked with colleagues in many countries, particularly France, Japan, Russia, Korea, and South America.[7]

He retired in 1979 but remained active as a scientist emeritus working with students and colleagues until his death in 1994. His namesake, *Alvin*, continues to help those scientists who came after him.

Robert Ballard

Robert Ballard

Discoverer of the *Titanic*

It is August 1973. Robert Ballard has just become the first American to dive into the deep Mid-Atlantic Ridge. Scientists are studying an area where the seafloor is spreading. As the French bathyscaphe (diving vessel) *Archimede* rises slowly from nine thousand feet under the ocean, Ballard smells smoke. Electrical wires are burning. Crew members reach for oxygen face masks. Ballard is getting no oxygen. He pulls the mask from his face, gasping for air. The two other crew members think he is panicking and try to put the mask back on him. Then Ballard draws his finger across his throat, the universal symbol that one is not getting air. Finally, a crew member realizes that Ballard's oxygen valve had not been turned on in the confusion of the fire. With that vital valve on, and other electrical switches off, the diving vessel safely returns to the surface.[1]

Ballard's dive to the Mid-Atlantic Ridge was just one of several important expeditions using deep submersibles he undertook for the Woods Hole Oceanographic Institution. In 1977, for example, Ballard was on a geological expedition off the Galapagos Islands, near Ecuador in the Pacific Ocean. Scientists were exploring an area of seafloor spreading, where molten lava from the earth's mantle periodically erupts and pushes the crust aside. This time they discovered that where the crust had been pushed apart, hydrothermal vents had formed in the cracks. Around these hot water springs, large white clams, tube worms, and other marine life clustered. How could life exist in this environment? Chemical tests showed the water coming up from the vents contained hydrogen sulfide. Scientists guessed that provided support for bacteria, which fed the marine life on the ocean bottom. Pictures of this undersea life were taken from cameras on both the *Alvin* submersible and an accompanying Acoustically Navigated Geophysical Underwater Survey (ANGUS), a camera system that could be towed by the mother ship.[2] Intrigued marine biologists returned two years later to see this undersea life for themselves. Among the things they saw were twelve-foot worms with no known close relatives.

In 1979 Ballard and *Alvin* discovered the now famous "black smokers" in the East Pacific. These huge chimneys are undersea geysers venting 662-degree black zinc sulfide steam from inside the earth.[3] Since these pioneer discoveries, further expeditions have increased our knowledge of the formation and movement of the ocean floor. Scientists continue to explore the sea to better understand the planet on which we live.

Geologist and deep-sea explorer Robert Duane Ballard was born in Wichita, Kansas, in 1942. His family moved to San Diego when he was still young. His father was a missile scientist with an aerospace company. "It was my father who taught me to take charge of my life," says Ballard. "I really believe that a person can be what he wants to be. As an under-graduate I was very goal oriented. I respect discipline. In my business you have to rely on the discipline of others."[4] Oceanographers at work in the sea depend on many members of the scientific team. They need designers of unique equipment to get them to the ocean floor, scientists to recognize and record the information they gather, and still others to help ana-lyze its meaning for the scientific community.

Ballard went through the Army's Reserve Officers Training Corps (ROTC) program at the University of California, Santa Barbara, and graduated with a bachelor's degree in physical sciences in 1965. He began work on his graduate degree in marine geology at the University of Hawaii. He also took a part-time job as a dolphin trainer at Sea Life Park. Ballard earned a commission as a second lieutenant in army intelligence, but he transferred to the navy during the Vietnam War.

In March 1967, Ballard and his new wife, Marjorie, drove to Boston. Ballard was to be the Navy liaison officer with the Woods Hole Oceanographic Institution. That September, he embarked on his first research cruise aboard the vessel *Chain.* The ship was using a high energy "sparker" to map the sea bottom at the edge of the continent. That meant a thunderous explosion took place every twenty seconds, twenty-four hours a day, for three weeks. The sparker was bouncing sound waves off the bottom. Such research expeditions require getting used to! In addition, such oceanographic instruments produce mountains of data. Ballard quickly learned that every day spent at sea later required a week's analysis.

Ballard's next endeavor required just such analysis. He began writing his first scientific paper. It was an analysis of depth sounding data collected in the Gulf of Mexico. Before the days of computers, depth soundings were recorded on long sheets of paper with thousands of marks. After months of labor and a major rewrite, Ballard's paper was published in the *Bulletin of Marine Science.*[5]

In September 1969, while mapping the geology of the Gulf of Maine, Ballard received a telephone call. His commander was calling to say that the navy was facing budget cuts. Ballard could either become a career officer or leave the Navy. He found a happy compromise. He was offered part-time work at

Woods Hole. He would also use his GI Bill to complete his doctorate in marine geology at the nearby University of Rhode Island. And he could retain his Navy reserve status.

Ballard's earliest dives using the submersible *Alvin* convinced him that it was an invaluable ocean research tool. After earning his Ph.D. in 1974, Ballard obtained navy funding for a one-year sabbatical (leave of absence with pay) at Stanford University. There he could write research papers based on his twelve years of explorations from Woods Hole. Stanford's location near high-tech Silicon Valley, however, showed him new opportunities:

> What I envisioned was a deep-towed vehicle carrying sensitive new video cameras. These would be connected to the surface by fiber-optic cable. Broadcast quality color TV images could be transmitted. Remote operation commands could be given. I began to design this new vehicle. The basic towed sled would be a remotely operated mother ship. It could launch a smaller exploration vehicle, also connected to the mother ship by fiber-optic cable. I planned to call my new vehicle the Argo-Jason system. I convinced my friend Sam Matthews of *National Geographic* to publish an illustration of this hypothetical system. Maybe I'd win development funding for the system.[6]

Ballard did win funding from the Navy for his *Argo-Jason* (now called *Medea-Jason*) idea. He gave a persuasive presentation about its potential wartime use. It could also investigate the sunken nuclear submarines *Thresher* and *Scorpion*, he argued. That navy assignment and its budget let Ballard establish the Deep Submergence Laboratory at Woods Hole. In addition to exploring the Navy's lost subs, Ballard had another dream. He wanted to find the *Titanic*, the "unsinkable" luxury liner that sunk on its maiden voyage in 1912. Ballard believed that finding it would show the historical research value of remotely operated vehicles like *Argo-Jason*. Some older colleagues thought such activities "inappropriate" for a geologist at a scientific institution. But they had also objected to *Alvin*—which some called the "toy submarine"—before it became in demand for research by scientists worldwide.

With painstaking work, Ballard and his crews explored the *Scorpion*. The *Titanic* was next! But only twelve days remained for the combined French-American expedition to find it. Three different reports of the location of the sunken ship existed from historical records. In addition, seventy-three years of undersea earthquakes and currents could have covered or scattered the light debris leading to the ship. The French had been unable to locate the wreck in the first phase of the search. Ballard's American crew persisted in tracking the seafloor in the area that they had calculated was the most likely location. They maintained round-the-clock watches, filming the bottom. Then, late one night a glimmer of metal appeared on the video screens. Was it part of

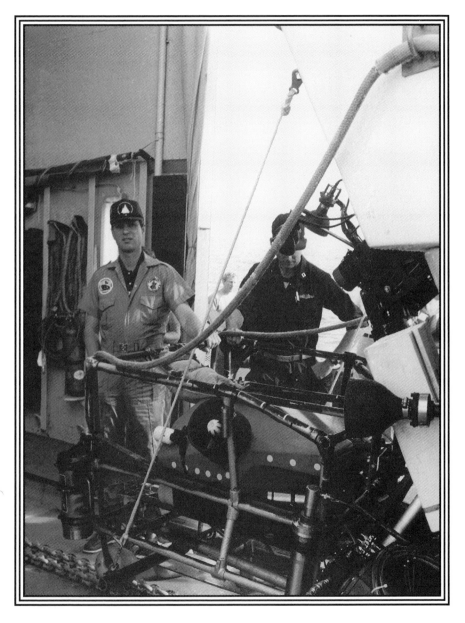

Ballard (left) helps a U.S. Navy deep submersible pilot conduct predive inspections on *Alvin* and *Jason Jr.*

the *Titanic*? Or was it one of the many ships sunk by German U-boats during World War II? At 1:05 A.M. the unmistakable image of one of the twenty-nine huge boilers confirmed their belief. They had found the *Titanic*! It was almost the same hour that the ship had sunk decades before. The *Titanic* had sunk at 2:20 A.M. on April 15, 1912.

Ballard's success on this French-American expedition became international news. It marked the beginning of further deep-sea historical explorations by Ballard. Best of all, Ballard found he could fulfill another dream. He founded the JASON project to bring the excitement of both science and exploration to middle school students. Through satellite hookups, students can watch explorations as they happen. Selected students can participate interactively to guide *Jason* as this remotely operated vehicle maps specific undersea targets. Scientists can show on the video screen the historical importance of artifacts. In a Mediterranean expedition, for example, marine archaeologist Dr. Anna Marguerite McCann showed cookware found on a sunken ship from the fourth century. The ship had sunk along a previously unknown trade route between Rome and Carthage. The discovery showed that ancient mariners traveled the open sea sooner than previously thought.[7] An April 1998 *National Geographic* article also described this expedition.

Robert and Marjorie Ballard had two sons, one of whom died in a car accident. In 1991 Ballard, who was then divorced, married Barbara Earle. Earle was in charge of National Geographic television specials and also worked with Ballard on his JASON project.

In 1997 Ballard retired from Woods Hole. Of all his explorations for that institution, he readily admits that the hydrothermal vents and the *Titanic* were his most exciting discoveries. His televised explorations have been seen by four hundred thousand science students. His television programs have been seen by millions more. But he isn't retiring from the ocean. He accepted an offer from the Mystic Aquarium in Connecticut to establish an Institute for Exploration. Referring to his new institute, Ballard says, "This will be the only aquarium that will have the ability to comprehensively show the ocean beneath 200 feet."[8] And Robert Ballard will also continue diving to bring back more answers to the ocean's mysteries.

Kathryn Sullivan

Kathryn Sullivan

Studying the Ocean from Space

On a shelf in Kathryn Sullivan's office sits a thimble-sized Styrofoam cup. It demonstrates that deep-sea pressure can crush a regular-size coffee cup—or a human. This remnant of a deep-ocean dive she made as a geologist in the submersible *Alvin* is a one-inch-high science lesson.

Science welcomes curious explorers. Oceanography and space are two fields where scientists work together as a team. Sullivan is an excellent example of what is now called earth system science. "By the 1980s," says Sullivan, "it became clear to scientists that ocean-atmosphere *interactions* are the most important things to learn about if we are to understand the earth as a *system*. The National Aeronautics and Space Administration (NASA) is a major player, along with oceanographers, in Earth System Science research."[1]

How did Sullivan become involved in earth system science?

"I first showed an interest in science during the second grade," says Sullivan. "My class did a series of simple, fun experiments." In high school, geography and languages became important too. In college, she chose earth sciences as her major. "None of my earlier study was wasted though. I found this new field offered many chances to travel. My foreign language training helped me read the scientific papers of European researchers."[2]

Kathryn Sullivan was born October 3, 1951, in Paterson, New Jersey, but grew up in California. Her bachelor's degree in earth sciences is from University of California, Santa Cruz. She earned her doctorate in geology at Dalhousie University in Nova Scotia in 1978. Sullivan did her earliest work for the United States Geological Survey on the 1973 Kelez Earthquake Investigation Expedition in the Pacific Ocean off the coast of southern California. Geologists and geophysicists on such expeditions explore the ocean floor looking for evidence of faults or fractures. By taking samples of the rocks on either side of such a fracture, they may discover a difference in the ages of the rocks, indicating that an earthquake dislocated the earth's crust in that area in the past—and may do so again in the future. This 1973 expedition discovered the Hosgri Fault System off Diablo Canyon in California, an underwater fault similar to the onshore and better-known San Andreas Fault.

That same year Sullivan went on an expedition into the Denmark Straits sponsored by the Canadian Bedford Institute of Oceanography. Her geological work there involved testing and evaluating a special camera and other tools for gathering samples from the ocean bottom. A second goal was to survey areas where manganese nodules might be forming. The voyage was part of a multinational program by the International Council for the Exploration of the Sea.

Sullivan's ocean studies in the mid-1970s focused on the Newfoundland Basin.

> I was interested in the geology of the North Atlantic. Those areas were formed many tens of millions of years ago. What is now Spain and Portugal were drifting apart from Canada through seafloor spreading. These research expeditions took me to Greenland and Iceland studying the earth's crust, its seamounts and ridge. Earlier I had been an ocean studies exchange student at the University of Bergen in Norway.

In 1974 Sullivan joined Project FAMOUS (the French-American Mid-Ocean Undersea Study) as a crew member working on paleomagnetic studies (study of the earth's magnetic field in earlier times).

It was very exciting to be working with scientists in my field like Jim Heirtzler, Jerry Van Andel, Tanya Atwater and Paul Johnson on this research expedition.

I didn't consider space as a career field until I was nearly finished with my doctoral work in geology. At that point, the space shuttle program was still under development. NASA wanted crew members who would serve as a mixture of flight engineer and chief scientist. This seemed similar to the role I had as a marine geologist aboard oceanic research vessels, so I applied.[3]

In 1978 Sullivan was selected from among sixty-five hundred applicants to be in the first class of space shuttle astronauts. She would be one of twenty mission specialists.

The job offer from NASA was an opportunity no earth scientist could pass up. My role aboard the space shuttle gave me two exciting exploration opportunities. One, I conducted experiments or observations for scientists and engineers on the ground. I served as their hands, eyes and ears in orbit. There's also a great responsibility here, too. Space flights are unique and expensive. Many events or observations only occur once during a flight. That means each procedure must be done correctly the first—and only—time. We must spend much time in training.

The second avenue of exploration is the one that motivated me to apply to NASA. The chance to look out my "office window" at the earth below.

It's hard to explain how magical an experience this is. The sweep of view and the detail are both remarkable. You're zooming past at about 18,000 miles an hour. There's no sound or wind, just the humming of the orbiter's fans and pumps. Inside the spacecraft, microgravity lets you literally float around the world. You float toward the windows for a look, with just the slightest push against a nearby seat or control panel.[4]

Sullivan flew in NASA's high-altitude research aircraft in 1978. She worked for two years on a variety of remote sensing projects involving radar and infrared thermal imaging (measuring the changing heat of the earth and its oceans). Her first space shuttle mission launched from the Kennedy Space Center in Florida on October 5, 1984. During the eight-day mission aboard the *Challenger*, the crew had to perform the following jobs seven hundred miles above the earth:

1. Measure how much radiation the earth receives, re-emits, and retains from the sun.
2. Find out how much energy is in the atmosphere, driving our weather systems.
3. Monitor air pollution.
4. Map ocean currents and the earth's underlying geology.
5. Conduct in-cabin experiments studying how humans adapt to weightlessness in space.

During this mission Sullivan became the first woman to spacewalk outside the shuttle. She and fellow crew member David C. Leestma conducted a three-and-a-half-hour test of special tools. These tools made it possible to refuel satellites on-orbit. What did it feel like taking that first step outside the shuttle? "You don't step, you 'swing' out," says Sullivan, "and you're excited to be getting on with the fun part of the job. You're also concentrating very hard so that you don't make mistakes."[5] Sullivan described her spacewalk job testing special tools this way:

> Imagine trying to refuel your car if one cap on the gas tank was crushed onto the tank mouth, a second one was screwed on and wired down, and the liquid coming from the fill hose was both extremely explosive and poisonous. You would need tools that simultaneously removed caps, connected the fuel line to the tank *and* isolated you very definitely from the liquid fuel.[6]

On that eight-day shuttle flight, Sullivan went around the world 192 times! On her third space shuttle mission, Sullivan served as payload commander. The ATLAS-1 (Atmospheric Laboratory for Applications and Science) mission obtained many detailed chemical and physical measurements.

To remain active in applied oceanography, Sullivan applied for a commission in the naval reserve after joining NASA. In 1990 she was selected to command an oceanography training unit at the naval air station in Dallas. She also worked in the Navy's Space and Naval War Command. Her many different jobs included providing environmental

Astronaut and oceanographer Kathryn Sullivan on a space mission.

support (weather and oceanography forecasts) to the Persian Gulf theater during Operation Desert Storm; conducting antisubmarine warfare operations in the Mediterranean; and offering support to combat exercises aboard the USS *Kitty Hawk* in the Pacific.

Her Navy and NASA jobs sometimes overlapped. While visiting the naval air station in Louisiana, Sullivan got a phone call from NASA's Mission Control. This concerned a problem aboard the space shuttle *Endeavor*. The crew members in orbit needed advice on how to fix a malfunctioning antenna on the shuttle. This was the same problem Sullivan had fixed during her 1984 spacewalk.

In a subsequent lecture to high school students in New Orleans, Sullivan gave career advice. She advised students to obtain as broad a science background as possible with a special emphasis on physics and math.[7]

In June 1993 Sullivan was appointed chief scientist at the National Oceanic and Atmospheric Administration (NOAA) by President Clinton, a position held earlier by Sylvia Earle. This new appointment involved directing NOAA's research and technology programs. As you can tell from its name, NOAA is involved with everything in the ocean and the atmosphere, including fish biology and stocks, global climate change, pollution, mapping and remote sensing.

After serving her term, Sullivan resigned in 1996. She was asked to become president of the Center of

Science and Industry (COSI) in Columbus, Ohio, a hands-on science center. COSI draws seven hundred thousand visitors annually. Education has always been a priority with Sullivan. As both an astronaut and a Navy officer, she spoke often to school and community groups. Nine years earlier she had created an educational program for the foundation established by the families of the *Challenger* 51-L crew. (This was the space shuttle carrying teacher Christa McAuliffe that exploded after takeoff.) The program she created for the Challenger Learning Centers is now in service at more than thirty locations in the United States and Canada.

Kathryn Sullivan's accomplishments are a testament to the value of education. She is a geologist, an oceanographer, and an astronaut. She is also a certified scuba diver, a private pilot, rated in both powered and glider aircraft, and she speaks five foreign languages. In commenting on Sullivan's new position at COSI, Senator John Glenn said, "There is no one better to teach children the wonders of science, than someone who is an astronaut and scientist herself."[8]

Chapter Notes

Chapter 1. Maurice Ewing: Mapping the Ocean Floor

1. William Wertenbaker, *The Floor of the Sea, Maurice Ewing and the Search to Understand the Earth* (Boston: Little, Brown, 1974), p. 23.

2. William B. F. Ryan, Lamont-Doherty Earth Observatory, correspondence with the author, May 18, 1998.

3. M. D. Candee, ed., *Current Biography* (New York: H. W. Wilson, 1953), pp. 188–189.

4. Wertenbaker, pp. 84–85.

5. Bridget Travers, ed., *World of Scientific Discovery* (Detroit: Gale Research, 1994), p. 234.

6. William B. F. Ryan, Lamont-Doherty Earth Observatory, correspondence with the author, January 16, 1998.

7. Wertenbaker, p. 170.

8. Sir Edward Bullard, "Introduction," in *Island Arcs, Deep Sea Trenches and Back-Arc Basins*, eds. Manik Talwani and Walter C. Pitman III (Washington, D.C.: American Geophysical Union, 1977).

Chapter 2. Ernest Everett Just: Understanding the Cell

1. James H. Kessler et al., eds., *Distinguished African American Scientists of the Twentieth Century* (Phoenix: Oryx Press, 1996), pp. 201–202.

2. Mary White Ovington, *Portraits in Color* (New York: Viking Press, 1927), pp. 162–163.

3. Kenneth R. Manning, *Black Apollo of Science: The Life of Ernest Everett Just* (New York: Oxford University Press, 1983), pp. 37–40.

4. Marine Biological Laboratory, Ernest Everett Just exhibit, 1996.

5. Louis Haber, *Black Pioneers of Science and Invention* (San Diego: Harcourt Brace, 1970), pp. 166–168.

6. Ovington, pp. 160–161.

7. Emily J. McMurray, ed., *Notable Twentieth-Century Scientists*, vol. 2 (Detroit: Gale Research, 1995), p. 1050.

8. Frank R. Lillie, *Science*, vol. 95, no. 2453, January 2, 1942, pp. 10–11.

9. Marine Biological Laboratory, Just exhibit.

10. Manning, pp. 304–330.

11. Kessler et al., p. 204.

12. Marine Biological Laboratory, Just exhibit.

Chapter 3. Sylvia A. Earle: Exploring and Explaining Marine Life

1. Sylvia A. Earle, *Sea Change: A Message of the Oceans* (New York: G. P. Putnam's Sons, 1995), pp. x–xii.

2. Marguerite Holloway, "Profile: Sylvia A. Earle," *Scientific American*, April 1992, p. 37.

3. Sylvia A. Earle, "Swimming with Humpback Whales," in *Animal People*, Gale Cooper (Boston: Houghton Mifflin, 1983), pp. 49, 51.

4. Earle, *Sea Change*, p. 60.

5. Ibid., pp. 67–70.

6. Sylvia A. Earle and Al Giddings, *Exploring the Deep Frontier* (Washington, D.C.: National Geographic Society, 1980), p. 231.

7. Earle, *Sea Change*, pp. 130–135.

8. "Chief Scientist at Federal Agency to Resign," *The New York Times*, January 19, 1992, Section 1, p. 18.

9. Earle, *Sea Change*, p. 326.

Chapter 4. Roger Revelle: Grandfather of the Greenhouse Effect

1. Dan Behrman, "Roger Revelle: A Practical Visionary," *Impact of Science on Society*, no. 156, 1989, p. 351.

2. Roger Revelle, "What Can We Do about Climate Change?" *Oceanography*, vol. 5, no. 2, 1992, pp. 126–127.

3. Judith and Neil Morgan, *Roger: A Biography of Roger Revelle* (San Diego: Scripps Institution of Oceanography, 1996), p. 16.

4. Roger Revelle, "How I Became an Oceanographer and Other Sea Stories," *Annual Review of Earth and Planetary Sciences*, vol. 15, 1987, pp. 4–5.

5. Morgan, pp. 22–23.

6. William A. Nierenberg, "Roger Revelle" (obituary), *Physics Today*, February 1992, p. 120.

7. Ibid.

Chapter 5. Walter Munk: Measuring Ocean Climate Worldwide

1. Walter Munk, "Affairs of the Sea," in *A Celebration in Geophysics and Oceanography, 1982* (La Jolla, Calif.: Scripps Institution of Oceanography, University of California, 1984), p. 4.

2. Ibid., p. 7.

3. Joseph Alper, "Munk's Hypothesis: A Slightly Mad Scheme to Measure Global Warming," *Sea Frontiers*, June 1991, p. 40.

4. Walter Munk, personal correspondence with the author, May 12, 1997.

5. Philip Yam, "Profile: Walter Munk," *Scientific American*, January 1995, p. 38.

6. Munk, "Affairs of the Sea," p. 6.

7. Walter Munk, personal interview with author, January 19, 1998.

8. Munk, "Affairs of the Sea," p. 20.

Chapter 6. Eugenie Clark: "The Shark Lady"

1. Eugenie Clark, "The Biggest Fish in the World," *Reader's Digest* Canadian edition, June 1993, pp. 100–105.

2. Eugenie Clark, *The Lady and the Sharks* (New York: Harper and Row, 1969), p. 3.

3. Pam Stacey, "Eugenie Clark: Without a Spear," *Calypso Log*, June 1990, p. 8.

4. Ibid.

5. Eugene K. Balon, "The Life and Work of Eugenie Clark: Devoted to Diving," *Environmental Biology of Fishes*, vol. 41, 1994, p. 93.

6. Eugenie Clark, "Expedition: Red Sea," *Sea Frontiers*, vol. 38, October 1992, p. 22.

7. Balon, pp. 96–98.

8. Clark, *The Lady and the Sharks*, p. 192.

9. Balon, pp. 100–101.

10. Eugenie Clark, "Into the Lairs of 'Sleeping' Sharks," *National Geographic*, vol. 147, no. 4, April 1975, pp. 570–584.

11. Eugenie Clark and Emory Kristof, as reported to Douglas Lee, "New Eyes for the Dark Reveal the World of Sharks at 2,000 Feet," *National Geographic*, vol. 170, no. 5, November 1986, p. 686.

12. Claudia Feldman, *Houston Chronicle*, February 20, 1996, Local section, p. 1.

Chapter 7. Henry Stommel: Understanding Ocean Circulation and Atmosphere

1. Paul R. Ryan, "Henry Stommel: 'Apprentice' Oceanographer," *Oceanus Magazine*, vol. 27, no. 1, Spring 1984, p. 56.

2. Arnold B. Arons, "The Scientific Work of Henry Stommel," in *Evolution of Physical Oceanography*, eds. Bruce A. Warren and Carl Wunsch (Cambridge, Mass.: The MIT Press, 1981), p. xiv.

3. Kirk Polking, *Oceans of the World: Our Essential Resource* (New York: Philomel, 1983), p. 13.

4. Arthur G. Gaines, Jr., *Ocean Frontiers* (New York: Harry N. Abrams, 1992), p. 73.

5. George Veronis, "A Theoretical Model of Henry Stommel," in *Evolution of Physical Oceanography*, eds. Bruce A. Warren and Carl Wunsch, p. xx.

6. Ibid., p. xxi.

7. Ibid., p. xxii.

8. Henry Stommel, *A View of the Sea* (Princeton, N.J.: Princeton University Press, 1987), pp. xi, 29–31.

9. Henry Stommel, "Why We Are Oceanographers," *Oceanography Magazine*, vol. 2, no. 2, November 1989, pp. 48–54.

10. Robert Kunzig, "A Thousand Diving Robots," *Discover Magazine*, April 1996, pp. 60–71.

11. Ryan, p. 59.

12. Henry Stommel, *Oceanus Magazine*, Spring 1984, p. 59.

Chapter 8. Allyn Vine: Pioneer of the Manned Deep-Sea Submersible

1. Sara L. Ellis, "Man of Vision," *Oceanus Magazine*, Winter 1988–1989, p. 65.

2. Victoria A. Kaharl, *Water Baby: The Story of Alvin* (New York: Oxford University Press, 1990), pp. 35–43.

3. Ellis, p. 63.

4. J. Lamar Worzel, "Allyn C. Vine" (obituary), *Physics Today*, November 1994, p. 106.

5. Kaharl, pp. 58–62.

6. Tom Gidwitz, "A Head Full of Ideas," *Ocean Explorer*, vol. 4, no. 1, September 1994, p. 6.

7. Mrs. Allyn Vine, personal correspondence with the author, June 2, 1997.

Chapter 9. Robert Ballard: Discoverer of the Titanic

1. Robert D. Ballard, *Explorations: My Quest for Adventure and Discovery Under the Sea*, with Malcolm McConnell (New York: Hyperion, 1995), pp. 127–128.

2. Robert D. Ballard, "The Exploits of Alvin and Angus: Exploring the East Pacific Rise," *Oceanus Magazine*, Fall 1984, pp. 7–14.

3. Ballard, *Explorations*, pp. 202–203.

4. Paul R. Ryan, "Robert D. Ballard: Deep Wilderness Man," *Oceanus Magazine*, Winter 1995–1996, pp. 120–121.

5. Ballard, *Explorations*, pp. 45–47.

6. Ibid., p. 207.

7. William J. Broad, "Secret Sub to Scan Seafloor for Roman Wrecks," *The New York Times*, February 7, 1995, p. C1.

8. Jonathan Rabinovitz, "Mystic Aquarium to Hire Leading Oceanographer," *The New York Times*, November 29, 1994, p. B6.

Chapter 10. Kathryn Sullivan: Studying the Ocean from Space

1. Kathryn D. Sullivan, correspondence with the author, January 30, 1998.

2. Kathryn D. Sullivan, "Foreword," in *Your Future in Space*, McPhee and Schulke (New York: Crown, 1986), p. 11.

3. Kathryn D. Sullivan, interview with the author, August 12, 1997.

4. Kathryn D. Sullivan, *Update*, Newsletter of the Geography Education Program, National Geographic Society, Fall 1991, p. 12.

5. Kathryn D. Sullivan, correspondence with the author, August 1997.

6. Kathryn D. Sullivan, correspondence with the author, June 1998.

7. Joe Darby, "Astronauts' Work Is Never Finished, Crew Woman Says They Do Groundwork for the Future," *New Orleans Times Picayune*, May 16, 1992, p. A16.

8. Ohio Center of Science and Industry, press release, February 14, 1996.

Resources

American Geophysical Union (AGU)
2000 Florida Ave. NW
Washington, DC 20009-1277
(800) 966-2481
fax: (202) 328-0566
e-mail: service@kosmos.agu.org
<http://www.agu.org>

American Society of Limnology
    and Oceanography (ASLO)
5400 Bosque Blvd., Suite 680
Waco, TX 76710-4446
(800) 929-2756
fax: (817) 776-3767
e-mail: business@aslo.org
<http://www.aslo.org/>

Consortium for Oceanographic
    Research and Education
1755 Massachusetts Ave. NW, Suite 800
Washington, DC 20036-2102
(202) 232-3900
fax: (202) 986-5072
e-mail: core@brook.edu
<http://core.cast.msstate.edu/corehmpg1.html>

National Association of Marine Laboratories
7 MBL St.
Water Street
Woods Hole, MA 02543
(508) 289-7405
fax: (508) 457-1924
e-mail: communications@mbl.edu
<http://www.mbl.edu/html/NAML/NAML.html>

National Sea Grant Office
NOAA/Sea Grant, R/ORI
1315 East-West Highway
SSMC-3, Eleventh Fl.
Silver Spring, MD 20910
(301) 713-2448
fax: (301) 713-0799
<http://www.mdsg.umd.edu/NSGO/index.html>

The Oceanography Society
4052 Timber Ridge Dr.
Virginia Beach, VA 23455
(757) 464-0131
fax: (757) 464-1759
e-mail: rhodesj@exis.net
<http://www.tos.org/>

Further Reading

Archbold, Rick. *Deep-Sea Explorer: The Story of Robert Ballard, Discoverer of the* Titanic. New York: Scholastic, 1994.

Berger, Melvin. *The Mighty Ocean: Student Book.* New York: Newbridge Educational Publishing, 1996.

Bett, Brian. *Planet Ocean.* Brookfield, Vt.: Ashgate Publishing, 1997.

Demuth, Patricia. *Way Down Deep: Strange Ocean Creatures.* New York: Putnam Publishing Group, 1995.

Fleisher, Paul. *Our Oceans: Experiments & Activities in Marine Science.* Brookfield, Conn.: Millbrook Press, 1995.

Franks, Sharon, and Judith Cohen. *You Can Be a Woman Oceanographer.* Seattle: Cascade Pass, 1994.

Haslam, Andrew, and Barbara Taylor. *Oceans.* Chicago: World Book, 1997.

Kerrod, Robin. *The Sea.* Milwaukee: Gareth Stevens, 1998.

Markle, Sandra. *Pioneering Ocean Depths.* New York: Simon & Schuster, 1995.

Mullican, Judith. *Under the Sea.* Mercer Island, Wash.: HighReach Learning, 1995.

Ocean Explorer. New York: D K Publishing, 1997.

Phillips, Francis, Gary Slater and Rob Shone. *The Ocean Deep.* Brookfield, Conn.: Millbrook Press, 1996.

Royston, Angela. *Under the Sea.* Portsmouth, N.H.: Heinemann Library, 1997.

Waters, John F. *Deep-Sea Vents: Living Worlds Without Sun.* New York: Dutton Children's Books, 1994.

Internet Addresses

Academy of Achievement
<http://www.achievement.org/>

Features profiles, interviews, and biographies of scientists, explorers, and others, including some of the individuals in this book.

Lamont-Doherty Earth Observatory
<http://www.ldeo.columbia.edu/Lamont.home.html>

Provides information about the observatory's research on oceans, climate, the environment, marine and other life, and earth science.

Monterey Bay Aquarium
<http://www.mbayaq.org/>

The E-Quarium gives a cyber-tour of the Monterey Bay's marine life, and the site provides information about ocean and atmospheric conditions, including El Niño.

Mystic Aquarium Institute for Exploration
<http://www.mysticaquarium.org/>

A major wellspring of research and education resources on oceanography, ocean exploration, and marine life.

Scripps Institution of Oceanography Library
<http://scilib.ucsd.edu/sio/>

Offers biographies and bibliographies of scientists associated with the institute.

Woods Hole Oceanographic Institute
<http://www.whoi.edu/>

Provides oceanography education resources and updates on the institute's research and marine operations.

Index

About the Author

Kirk Polking is a freelance author of nonfiction books for children and adults. Her previous books for children covered the expeditions of Lewis and Clark and Henry Hudson, how laws are made in Congress, and the peaceful uses of atomic energy. She has previously written a book on oceanography titled *Oceans of the World: Our Essential Resource.* Her books for adults include *The Private Pilot's Dictionary and Handbook* and a dozen books on writing, the most recent of which is *Writing Family Histories and Memoirs.*

3/01

NEW HANOVER COUNTY PUBLIC LIBRARY
201 Chestnut Street
Wilmington, N.C. 28401

GAYLORD R

ML